Vera Lex

Journal of the International Natural Law Society

New Series Volume 1, Numbers 1&2 Winter 2000

Pace University Press
1 Pace Plaza
New York, NY 10038

ISBN 0-944473-53-9

CONTRIBUTORS
Address all submissions and correspondence to The Editor, VERA LEX, Pace University, Department of Philosophy & Religious Studies, 1 Pace Plaza, New York, NY 10038. Please send two copies of the paper submitted. Include adequate margins, double space everything (text, notes, works cited, quotations). Use U.S. spelling and punctuation style, (e.g. periods inside quotation marks; "double quotes" for opening and closing quotations). The University of Chicago Manual of Style, 13th Edition, is to be consulted regarding matters of style. Notes are to be numbered consecutively (in Arabic numerals) and placed at the bottom of the page.

SUBSCRIBERS
VERA LEX is published annually by Pace University Press, 1 Pace Plaza, New York, NY 10038. Subscription price: $40 for libraries and institutions; $25 for individuals. Please send all subscription inquiries to The Editor.

INDEXING AND ABSTRACTING
VERA LEX is indexed in *Philosopher's Index*.

VERA LEX *the journal of the International Natural Law Society was established to communicate and dialogue on the subject of natural law and natural right, to introduce natural law philosophy into the mainstream of contemporary thought and to strengthen the current revived interest in the discussion of morals and law and advance its historical research.*

Why do we use a shell (*Nautilus pomplilus Linnaeus*) to symbolize *vera lex*? The logarithmic spiraling and overlapping chambers of the shell are endless. They suggest a patterned development and evolution that, by its radial and circular design, never comes to an end. This means that the shell is at once specific and real, while its form, like law, is abstract and ideal.

The pattern of a shell is, like good law, uniform, regular and reliable. It can therefore be anticipated and known. The pattern of a shell is balanced, like justice. *Una iustitia.*

A shell is a biological being. Like law, it has life and dynamic. It grows. (There is an average of thirty growth lines per chamber, one for every day in the lunar cycle, suggesting that a new chamber is put down each lunar month and a new growth line each day, thus recording two different natural rhythms, lunar and solar.)

The shell is a universal and common object known to everyone. A shell is not soft tissue easily destroyed. And yet, like liberty, it is fragile in certain respects if stepped on with an iron boot. It has to be guarded with vigilance or it is crushed.

In every shell lives a nautilus. If the shell is law, the nautilus (snail) is a person—it is alive—person and law. Their destinies, like person and law, are interdependent.

Vera Lex

leges innumerae, una iustitia

Contents

New Series Volume 1, Numbers 1 & 2 **Winter 2000**

EDITORIAL

This issue of VERA LEX is the first one under my editorship. Undoubtedly you will notice some changes mainly cosmetic; this is a reflection more of different aesthetic dispositions than any substantive differences between the editors. Hopefully the content remains within the high standard established over twenty years by the past editor and founder Virginia Black. I wish to thank Virginia for her guidance and inspiration and I hope to continue her tradition of excellence.

As we go to press signs of environmental desiccation are accumulating rapidly. Global warming for example: the North Pole is defrosting; researchers have identified a potent anthropogenic greenhouse gas SF5CF3; Northern Hemisphere sea ice is melting at a rate of approximately fifteen feet per decade. According to the *New York Times* (8/28), U. S. federal judges are systematically bribed by corporations with a vested interest in the deregulation of environmental law. Yellow River dolphins are near extinction and are likely to be extinct by the next decade due to the Three-Gorge Dam project (the largest hydroelectric project ever undertaken). Large portions of western U. S. forests are ablaze because of poor logging practices. Progress in nano-technology, human eugenics and genetic engineering are changing 'nature' in dangerous ways, while seriously threatening democratic processes. Poverty, pollution and growing populations are accepted as necessary adjuncts to economic progress and prosperity.

Sadly, we know this litany too well and undoubtedly each of us could provide additional examples. In the past this journal has added to the literature on such topics as dignity, equity, autonomy and liberty in relation to natural law. In that tradition the current issue of *Vera Lex* explores ways in which natural law can meaningfully enter the conversation about urgent environmental concerns. The first article challenges the widely held belief that natural law theory as an aspect of the Judeo-Christian tradition lacks the necessary resources for a non-anthropocentric environmental ethic. Prof. Cvek demonstrates that the natural law position of Thomas Aquinas—a prominent target for criticism by environmental philosophers—has much that is positive to contribute to the discussion about environmental value. Cvek argues convincingly for what he calls "nonegalitarian biocentrism" in Aquinas' natural law theory. Although this position does not constitute the moral community that some philosophers require for dismantling anthropocentrism, it does go far in diffusing the claim that only humans possess the value necessary for moral consideration.

If Cvek's article is more theoretical and provides justification for using natural law in response to environmental issues, Frank Derringh's article attempts to "apply" natural law theory to a fundamental environmental problem and finds it lacking. Professor Derringh argues that certain natural law theories (Aquinas and Finnis) are inadequate when it comes to limiting procreation, and by extension limiting human intervention in the world of nature. By grafting more biological/ecological (read Darwinian) premises onto traditional natural law theory (in a manner similar to Arnhart—see this issue for a review of his book) Derringh believes natural law theorists can answer their influential critics. Thomas Spademan provides a cogent attempt at applying natural law to environmental concerns, specifically economic externalities caused by business activities. Prof. Spademan argues that businesses have neglected broader social duties because they lack a coherent theory for prioritizing them and natural law can provide such a theory. Building on Aquinas's natural law theory and Richard Wasserstrom's legal ethics, Spademan constructs a taxonomy based on natural law that distinguishes between "role duties" and broader social duties and demonstrates when social duties trump role duties.

Finally, Prof. Guido Leidig invites us to consider natural law as a foundation for a multidisciplinary approach to environmental issues. The framework for this multidisciplinary discourse consists of ecology (natural sciences), economics (social sciences) and jurisprudence (philosophy of law/legal theory). According to Prof. Leidig, "...current and scientifically interesting problem areas in...environmental policy cannot be discussed with finality without a philosophical basis in natural law." This is because there is very little overlap between two major systems: the ecologic and the anthropogenic. According to the author, natural law has the potential to unify these often disparate systems, but only if it can accommodate some version of chaos theory. We also included an article by Alejandra Carrasco, "Practical Reason, Person and the Common Good." Although this has little to do directly with the theme of this issue it is an important addition to the philosophy of natural law and the careful reader will certainly find points of connection between it and our theme.

A number of the authors featured here recognize the importance of natural law in addressing ecological/environmental problems, but express concern about its ability to succeed without input from other disciplines—Arnhart's position relies heavily on Humean and Darwinian notions of social sentiments as adjuncts to the precepts of natural law and, in like mannner, Derringh suggests a biologically-grounded natural law. Of course, important questions remain as to how much input from other disciplines/sources before natural law is disfigured beyond recognition, but this is a fine beginning for the topic of natural law and its relation to environmental thought.

FEATURES

THOMAS AQUINAS, NATURAL LAW, AND ENVIRONMENTAL ETHICS

Peter P. Cvek

Most contemporary ethicists view the Judeo-Christian moral tradition as an obstacle to the development of an ethics of the environment.[1] Within this moral tradition, the negative attitude toward the natural environment is typically illustrated by the claim of human superiority over the rest of nature, as well as the apparent lack of concern for the treatment of nonhuman animals. In the words of Genesis 1, 26, God made humanity in His own image and likeness, and gave to humanity dominion over the earth and all of its creatures. This divine grant of dominion has been broadly construed in terms of an almost absolute right to use the things of the earth, including nonhuman animals, for the satisfaction of human needs.

As part of the Judeo-Christian tradition, the Natural Law philosophy of Thomas Aquinas seems to be equally infected with the same lack of concern for animals and nature characteristic of the whole tradition. In fact, according to Daniel Dombrowski, "the intellectual framework that supports the dominant Christian view of animals is best exhibited in the writings of Thomas Aquinas."[2] Dombrowski concludes, like many other contemporary critics, that "the Judeo-Christian tradition, even for a sophisticated thinker like St. Thomas, has largely been speciesist."[3]

The philosophy of Thomas Aquinas certainly appears to be committed to the belief that only human beings are fitting subjects of moral concern, and thus a perfect example of what is now called "speciesism" or "anthropocentrism."[4] At the core of the anthropocentric world-view is the assumption that only human beings possess intrinsic moral value. In the

[1]John Passmore, "The Treatment of Animals," *Journal of the History of Ideas*, 37, 2, (1975), 195-209.

[2]Daniel Dombrowski, *Hartshorne and the Metaphysics of Animal Rights*, (Albany, NY: State University of New York Press, 1998), 9.

[3]Daniel Dombrowski, (1988), 10.

[4]See Roderick Frazier Nash, *The Rights of Nature: A History of Environmental Ethics*, (University of Wisconsin Press, 1989).

Thomistic Natural Law context, only rational (human) beings are properly subject to the natural (moral) law, or, what amounts to the same thing, only human beings are members of the moral community. Combined with the doctrine of the hierarchy of being, the belief that reality is structured according to various levels of perfection, ranging from God, through angels, humanity, animals, plants, and inanimate matter, this decidedly anthropocentric claim constitutes the main philosophical basis for humanity's claim to dominion over the earth and all its creatures. For, in this hierarchy, each being occupies its proper place and exists to serve the beings that are above it. Animals, plants, and the earth itself have only instrumental value. They are the means ordained to serve human ends, in accordance with the order of nature and the will of God.

The general purpose of this paper is to challenge the dominant anthropocentric interpretation of the Thomistic theory of natural law. I will suggest that the moral philosophy of Thomas Aquinas is not inherently opposed to the concerns of contemporary environmentalists. In particular, I will argue that, within the traditional doctrine of natural law, there is the foundation for an ethics of the environment, which has been overshadowed by the dominance of the anthropocentric reading.[5]

The paper is divided into two parts. The first part will consider the extent to which the Thomistic theory of natural law is an instantiation of anthropocentrism. I will show that although Aquinas assumes that human beings are uniquely related to the natural law, he still insists that all living beings are subject to the natural law, and thus worthy of some degree of respect. The second part of the paper will examine the Thomistic understanding of the hierarchy of being. I will suggest that, contrary to the standard account, Aquinas is best understood as an advocate of a "nonegalitarian biocentrism," that is, a mean between the extremes of egalitarian biocentrism and anthropocentrism.

NATURAL LAW AND ANTHROPOCENTRISM

What is Thomas Aquinas' understanding of the moral status of animals? Those commentators most sympathetic to Thomistic natural law ethics have been vigorous in their exclusion of animals from the moral

[5]For a general discussion, see Peter S. Wenz, *Environmental Justice*, (State University of New York Press, 1989), chapter 13, 271-309.

community. For example, Joseph Rickaby, S. J., in his *Moral Philosophy or Ethics and Natural Law* (1901), summarizes the Thomistic position in unequivocal terms:

> Brute beasts, not having understanding and therefore not being persons, cannot have any rights. The conclusion is clear. They are not autocentric. They are of the number of *things*, which are another's : They are chattels, or cattle. We have no duties to them; not of justice, as is shown; not of religion, unless we are to worship them, like the Egyptians of old; not of fidelity, for they are incapable of accepting a promise. . .We have (then) no duties of charity, nor duties of any kind, to the lower animals, as neither to stocks nor stones. . .Brutes are as *things* in our regard: so far as they are useful to us, they exist for us, not for themselves; and we do right in using them unsparingly for our need and convenience, though not for our wantonness.[6]

This traditional understanding of the moral status of animals leaves little room for a relation to nature that is not based on domination and exploitation. But is this anthropocentrism really a necessary feature of the Thomistic doctrine of natural law?

In so far as Aquinas believes that only rational (human) beings are subject to the natural law, his ethical outlook would seem to be wholly anthropocentric. William May, for instance, voices the standard position when he argues that, for Aquinas, law, in its normative sense, is something which pertains in a unique way to human intelligence.[7] This interpretation seems to be confirmed in the *Summa Theologica*. Aquinas initially describes law as "a rule and measure of acts, whereby man is induced to act or restrained from acting."[8] Since the rule governing voluntary human acts is reason, Aquinas insists that law must be something which pertains to intelligence. Since law and morality are the exclusive products of reason, only rational beings are subject to the moral law in the proper sense of the term. Nonrational beings are thus necessarily excluded from the realm of law and morality.

[6]Joseph Rickaby, S.J., *Moral Philosophy or Ethics and Natural Law*, (London: Longmans, Green, and Co., 1901), 248-50.

[7]William E. May, "The Meaning and Nature of the Natural Law in Thomas Aquinas," *The American Journal of Jurisprudence*, 22, (1977), 173.

[8]Thomas Aquinas, *Summa Theologica*, I-II, 90, 1. All further references will be made in the text.

There are, however, reasons for doubting the accuracy of this anthropocentric restriction in the scope of the natural law. Throughout his discussion of law, Aquinas repeatedly makes room for the definition of Ulpian, according to which "natural law is that which all animals have been taught by nature," and which continues "this law is not peculiar to the human species, it is common to all animals which are produced on land or sea, and to fowls of the air as well."[9] The inclusion of this reference is all the more peculiar in light of the fact that Aquinas' mentor, Albert the Great, expressly rejected the very same description of natural law, since it seemed to contradict the claim that law is exclusively a product of reason. This peculiarity, however, disappears once Aquinas' conception of natural law is viewed from within its broader context, that is, as a subset of the Eternal Law.

What Aquinas calls the "eternal law" is the intellectual understanding of the created order in the mind of God. Eternal law "regulates" the entire created universe and directs each thing toward its proper end. This divinely ordained teleological order is promulgated throughout nature by the very fact of creation. All created beings, both rational and nonrational, are governed by the eternal law, because all beings can be seen to act for an end.[10] This similarity between rational and nonrational beings is an essential part of the eternal law, which is revealed in and through the teleological structure of the natural order.

Aquinas makes this similarity clear in the *Summa Contra Gentiles*: ". . .for every agent the principle of its action is either its nature or its intellect."[11] Of course, there is no doubt that intellectual agents act for the sake of an end, because they think ahead of time of the things which they

[9]*The Digest of Justinian*, cited by Aquinas, *Summa Theologica* I-II, 94, 2 and elsewhere. For the Thomistic discussion, see M. B. Crowe, "St. Thomas and Ulpian's Natural Law," *St. Thomas Aquinas 1274-1974 Commemorative Studies* (Toronto: Pontifical Institute of Mediaeval Studies, 1974), 261-282, and William May (cited in note 7).

[10]"Now just as man, by such a pronouncement, impresses a kind of inward principle of action on the man subject to him, so God imprints on the whole of nature the principles of its proper actions. . .And thus all actions and movements of the whole of nature are subject to the eternal law. Consequently, irrational creatures are subject to the eternal law through being moved by the divine providence; but not, as rational creatures are, through understanding the divine commandment." (S.T., I-II, 93, 6).

[11]Compare with *Summa Contra Gentiles* (3.75.4): Singulars are governed "by the use of reason in the case of men, and by means of natural instinct in the cases of bees and

wish to achieve through action; and their action is based on this preconception. This is what it means for the intellect to be the principle of action.

> Just as the entire likeness of the result achieved by the actions of an intelligent agent exists in the intellect that preconceives it, so, too, does the likeness of a natural resultant pre-exist in the natural agent; and as a consequence of this, the action is determined to a definite result. . . Therefore, the agent that acts with nature as its principle is just as much directed to a definite end, in its action, as is the agent that acts through intellect as its principle. Therefore, every agent acts for an end. (S.G. 2.2.8)

Moreover, "If an agent did not incline toward some definite effect, all results would be a matter of indifference for him" (S.G. 3.2.8). But it is readily apparent that some effects are better than others. Put differently, the end for the sake of which an agent acts must be a good for that agent. For, "that toward which an agent tends toward in a definite way must be appropriate to it, because the agent would not be inclined to it except by virtue of some agreement with it. But, what is appropriate to something is good for it" (S.G. 3.3.2). So, every agent, whether intellectual or natural, acts for an end, which is a good for that agent.

It is in virtue of this common teleological orientation, that all created beings are said to be subject to or "participate in" the eternal law. But, as noted above, their participation differs in accordance with their natures. Rational beings participate consciously in the eternal law. By rationally reflecting on their own natural inclinations, human beings are able to apprehend the ends or purposes of those inclinations and thereby promulgate the natural law to themselves. In other words, rational agents act by considering the rational character of the good and allowing that meaning to motivate their will. Nonrational beings, in contrast, are determined to their proper end by natural appetite alone (S.G. 3.3.7). As Aquinas observes, nonrational beings participate in the eternal law unconsciously or instinctually, "namely, from it being imprinted on them, they derive their respective inclinations to their proper acts and ends"(S.T. I-II, 91, 2).

---

many brute animals that are governed by some sort of natural instinct. . .(God's will) is universally concerned with every good thing. . ."

Since nonrational beings do not participate in the eternal law in a rational manner, their participation is said to be "by way of likeness" or similitude. However, it is important to remember that, in contrast to the anthropocentric reading, this reference to an analogous form of participation is not meant to deny that nonrational beings participate in the rational order of nature. Quite the contrary, the account of these two distinct, but similar, forms of participation is intended to explain and reinforce the belief that all beings are subject to the natural law in their own way, and thus have natural ends or goods toward which they are directed by both God and nature.

This similitude between nature and humanity is poignantly illustrated in Aquinas' discussion of how human beings promulgate the natural law to themselves. Since every agent acts for an end, which has the nature of good, the role of practical reason is to direct actions in accordance with its apprehension of what is truly good. The first formal principle of practical reason is founded on the conception of the good, as that which all things seek after by nature. Accordingly, good is to be done and promoted, and evil is to be avoided. The content of the principles or precepts of natural law are founded on this formal principle. These principles are discovered by practical reason as it reflects on those tendencies or inclinations inherent in nature. The order of these precepts is based on the order of natural inclinations. First, human beings along with all natural beings, share a common inclination to preserve themselves in existence. The preservation of life is thus a precept of the natural law. Secondly, there is an inclination possessed in common with all animals, that is, "which nature has taught all animals," such as sexual intercourse and the education of offspring (S.T. I-II, 94, 2). The ends of this natural inclination are thus recognized as goods which, not only animals do pursue by nature, but which they ought to pursue. Thirdly, because human beings are rational by nature, they possess an inclination to know the truth about God and to live in society. These goods are thus unique to human nature.

In sum, natural inclinations direct all beings to their natural ends. These ends are indicative of what is good for that being. Since rational beings are capable of knowing these ends or goods, and relating means to ends, they are under an obligation to seek and pursue what is good. Analogously, nonrational beings are also directed to their proper ends. But while rational beings apprehend and freely will their own good, nonrational beings pursue their respective goods by the necessity of their natures. In either case, the common foundation for the analogy is that all beings are teleologically directed to that good which is proper to their nature.

This common teleological orientation implies that all activities, both internal and external to the being, can be evaluated in terms of the extent to which they contribute or fail to contribute to the realization of the being's own good. Although different goods are proper to different beings, all beings share one common good, that of life or self-preservation. As Aquinas notes, "the very fact of being is a good, and so all things desire to be. [Thus] every action and movement [can be] seen to be ordered in some way toward being, either that it may be preserved in the species or in the individual, or that it may be newly acquired" (S.G. 3.3.4). Aquinas even observes that nature is arranged to further this end, for "in each species there are provided the means whereby any individual of the species may be preserved in being" (S.G. 3.3.8). For example, "in the plant world leaves are arranged so as to protect the fruit, and among animals the bodily organs are disposed in such a way that the animal can be protected" (S.G. 3.3.9).

Much of this talk of natural teleology might seem irrelevant to contemporary ethical debate, were it not for the emergence of a teleological orientation among many environmental ethicists. According to Paul Taylor, who is perhaps the best example of this trend, the attitude of respect for nature is based on, what he calls, the Biocentric outlook on nature.[12] This biocentrism is based on four claims: (1) the common membership of all living beings in the Earth's Community of Life, (2) the interdependence of all living beings, (3) the claim that all living beings are teleological centers of life, and (4) the denial of human superiority over other living beings.

Claims (1) and (2) focus on the common characteristics and similar basic requirements for survival faced by all biological life. By and large, Aquinas would formally agree with these two claims, although his acceptance of the hierarchy of being might suggest a disagreement about the

[12]Paul Taylor, *Respect for Nature: A Theory of Environmental Ethics*, (Princeton University Press, 1986), 99-100.

structure of interdependence. More importantly, he would certainly agree with (3), the claim that each organism is a "teleological center of life," that is, an organized center of activity which is striving to preserve itself and realize its own good in its own unique way. According to Taylor,

> To say that it is a teleological center of life is to say that its internal functioning as well as its external activities are all goal-oriented, having the constant tendency to maintain the organism's existence through time and to ensure it successfully to perform those biological operations whereby it reproduces its kind and continually adopts to changing environmental events and conditions. It is the coherence and unity of these functions of an organism, all directed toward the realization of its good, that make it one teleological center of activity.[13]

As should be readily apparent, this teleological conception of living beings is certainly consistent with the Thomistic understanding of the natural order. Like Aquinas, this applies to both rational and nonrational beings. As Taylor notes, viewing organisms in this way does not entail the possession of consciousness on the part of the organism, it does not imply that it is intentionally aiming at some end, or even aware of what it is doing. Whether conscious or not, all organisms can be said to be teleological centers of life in that "each is a unified, coherently ordered system of goal-oriented activities that has a constant tendency to protect and maintain the organism's existence."[14]

Aquinas could not ask for a better statement of his own teleological understanding of nature. However, Aquinas would supposedly object to (4), the denial of human superiority over other living beings. In contrast with Taylor's egalitarianism, in which all living beings are equally worthy of respect, as ends in themselves, Aquinas seems committed to a hierarchical order, within which human beings may use nonrational beings as means to their own ends.

THE HIERARCHY OF BEING

In the *Summa Contra Gentiles*, Aquinas notes that there is "a natural desire common to all things by which they desire their own preservation, to the extent that it is possible" (S.G. 3.63.8). Human beings, of course,

[13]Taylor, 121-22.
[14]Taylor, 122.

are morally obliged to preserve themselves and other human beings. If nonrational beings also naturally pursue the good of self-preservation, then, what duties do rational beings have to promote the good of nonrational beings? In the context of the hierarchy of being, Aquinas is hesitant to ascribe moral duties toward nonrational beings. This reluctance has certainly been responsible for much of the negative assessment of natural law's prospects for providing an adequate environmental ethics. But, why is Aquinas so unwilling to prescribe duties toward nonrational beings?

Considering the possible moral relationship between rational and nonrational beings, Aquinas asks: "Whether irrational creatures are to be loved out of charity?" Interpreting charity (caritas) as love or friendship, he concludes that one cannot exercise "friendship" toward nonrational creatures. Three reasons are advanced to support this conclusion:

> 1) Friendship means wanting one's friend's good, but nonrational creatures "do not properly have a good" because they lack reason and freedom of choice.
> 2) Friendship is based on community of life, but nonrational creatures cannot have community with "human life which is in accordance with reason."
> 3) Friendship is ultimately founded on a community of eternal happiness, for which nonrational creatures have no capability.
> (S.T. II-II, 25, 3)

All three of these reasons are variations on the same anthropocentric theme. Putting aside (3), which depends on a theological extension of the thesis, the argument depends on determining the prerequisites for membership in the moral community. Nonrational beings cannot be objects of human friendship or charity, that is, they cannot be proper objects of moral concern, because they are not full-fledged members of the moral community. Membership in the moral community requires the possession of reason and the capacity for free choice. More precisely, it requires the capacity for moral agency. As Aquinas points out, "since intellectual creatures possess reason and free will, and thus have dominion over their own acts, providence cares for them for their own sake" (S.G. 3.1.112). Because nonrational beings lack this capacity, they are excluded from the moral community. Aquinas further concludes that such beings are rightly subject to the rational will of another, for, "things which have no dominion over their acts are cared for, not for their own sake, but for the sake of others" (S.G. 3.1.112).

It is worth noting that the exclusion of nonrational beings from the moral community is not because of some obsession with rationality as such, but because reason is the necessary condition for being a moral agent. When Aquinas asserts that nonrational beings "do not properly have a good," he is merely observing that nonrational beings, because they lack reason and free will, are not moral agents. They are compelled by nature to seek their own natural good, without the benefit of reason or free choice. In contrast, rational beings intellectually apprehend their natural good and freely choose to pursue or avoid it: it is for them a moral end. For this reason, their actions are either right or wrong, and as agents their conduct can be subject to moral evaluation.[15] As recently explained by Tom Regan, moral agents "not only can do what is right or wrong, they may also be on the receiving end, so to speak, of the right or wrong acts of other moral agents."[16] There is, therefore, a reciprocity between moral agents. It is this reciprocity of rights and duties between moral agents which constitutes the moral community. In contrast, nonrational beings appear to be, what Tom Regan calls, "moral patients."[17] Moral patients lack reason and will, and therefore lack the capacity for moral agency. Since they cannot apprehend an end as a good or calculate means to this end, let alone act by free choice, they cannot be said to do what is right or wrong, in the moral sense. Nor, it seems, can they be on the receiving end of the right or wrong acts of moral agents. Or, at least this is the con-

[15]The distinction at issue here is that between a moral good and a natural good. Put simply, a natural good is that which a living being seeks by nature, a moral good is a natural good which is grasped by practical reason. Whether or not this distinction really makes a difference is still a debating point among contemporary Thomists. For many Thomists, practical reason merely demands that we pursue what is naturally good. See Germain Grisez, "The First Principle of Practical Reason: A Commentary on the *Summa Theologica*, I-II. q. 94, a. 2," *The Natural Law Forum*, 10 (1965), 168-201; John Finnis, *Natural Law and Natural Rights* (Oxford, 1980).

[16]Tom Regan, *The Case for Animal Rights*, (University of California Press, 1983), 152.

[17]Tom Regan, (1983), 151-54.

clusion taken for granted by Aquinas. Since nonrational beings cannot engage in the reciprocity of moral activity, they cannot be active members of the moral community.

Since both rational and nonrational beings are directed toward the same natural good of preservation, this exclusion of nonrational beings from the moral community requires closer examination. Even if we agree that nonrational beings cannot be moral agents, it is not clear why we ought not be concerned about their good as moral patients. Certainly, the inability to engage in reciprocal moral action is not a sufficient reason for the blanket exclusion of nonrational beings from the scope of our moral concern. So, why are we not obliged to seek to further the natural good of all living beings?

It is at this point that the traditional anthropocentric interpretation would appeal to the hierarchy of being to explain why the good of nonrational beings may be subordinated to the good of rational beings. However, even this appeal is not without its qualifications. One minor adjustment is reflected in the distinction between direct and indirect duties. Although nonrational beings cannot be the direct objects of charity, they can be its indirect objects.[18] They can be "loved out of charity as goods that we want for others; insofar as, out of charity, we want to preserve them to the honor of God and the utility of human beings"(S.T. II-II, 25, 3). At first this seems to be just another extension of the anthropocentric thesis. We ought to be concerned for nonrational beings because they have an instrumental value for ourselves and other human beings. For example, I have a duty not to harm my neighbor's pet dog, not because I have a duty to the animal, but because I have a duty to respect my neighbor's property. The animal in question is merely the indirect

[18]Indeed, if any statements are found in Sacred Scripture prohibiting the commission of an act of cruelty against brute animals, for instance, that one should not kill a bird accompanied by her young (Deut. 22:6), this is said either to turn the mind of man away from cruelty which might be used on other men, lest a person through practicing cruelty on brutes might go on to do the same to men; or because an injurious act committed on animals may lead to a temporal loss for some man, either for the agent or for another man; or there may be another interpretation of the text, as the Apostle (I Cor. 9:9) explains it, in terms of "not muzzling the ox that treadeth the corn" (Deut. 25:4)." *Summa Contra Gentiles*, 3.112.13.

beneficiary of my direct duty to another human being. But the reference to God suggests a much broader point. We ought to seek the preservation of nonrational beings for the sake of the honor of God. Exactly what this entails is not immediately evident. Nevertheless, Aquinas provides ample clues.

For Aquinas, as we have seen, the entire natural order is a reflection of the eternal law in the mind of God. Every created being has its own specific good toward which it is directed by the necessity of its own nature and in accordance with the provident will of God. From the divine perspective, all of creation is good and every being, at its own level, contributes to the overall goodness and ordered perfection of creation as a whole. In a rather anthropocentric comment about nonrational beings, Aquinas notes that "if the things needed for the perfection of intellectual substances were lacking, the universe would not be complete" (S.G. 3.112.8). At the same time, Aquinas notes that "it is not contradictory for some natures to be for the sake of intellectual ones, and also for the sake of the perfection of the universe" (S.G. 3.112.8). This conjunction of natural subordination and the perfection of the universe is the basis of Aquinas' nonegalitarian biocentric understanding of the proper moral relationship between humanity and nature.

While Aquinas insists that nonrational beings have an instrumental value for human agents, this is not meant to exhaust their value. On the one hand, humanity's dominion does include the right to exercise power over nonrational beings. In general, this dominion consists in the power to make use of things for the support of human life (S.T. II-II. 66, 1). Accordingly, the primary example of use is for food (S.T. II-II 64, 1). On the other hand, this right to use individual nonrational beings to satisfy legitimate human needs is correlated with, and conditioned by, a duty to respect the ultimate purpose of creation and divine providence.

From the divine perspective, all beings are good, and the life of every being has value. All beings, rational and nonrational, exist for the sake of the perfection of the universe. Moreover, since all beings contribute to the common good and perfection of the natural order as a whole, divine providence has ordained that, as much as possible, all beings should be preserved in existence (S.G. 3.65). Accordingly, human beings have a duty to seek the preservation of the natural order, at least with respect to the preservation of each natural species.[19] Even if this is construed as a direct duty to God, and thus an indirect duty to nonrational beings, it is a duty which transcends the narrow limits of strict anthropocentrism, since it requires that every natural species be preserved independent of each individual's possible instrumental value for human beings, that is, for the sake of the perfection of the universe as a whole. Put differently, this duty assumes that every natural species is to be preserved in virtue of its necessary relationship to the completeness and perfection of the natural order. Perhaps inadvertently, this duty, in effect, captures Taylor's second biocentric claim with respect to the interconnectedness of all living beings. Aquinas' position is thus indicative of a holistic ethics of the environment, wherein "our conduct with regard to the natural world is right if it tends to preserve the ecological stability, integrity, and equilibrium of biotic communities, and wrong if it tends to destroy or disrupt such ecological balance."[20]

CONCLUSION

In accordance with a comment by Andrew Linzey, "the problem with Aquinas. . .is not his notion of an overarching divine order, but his oversimplification. . .of what constitutes this divine order."[21] In his determination to avoid the erroneous view of the Manicheans/Albigensians, who maintained that the killing of animals was always impermissable, Aquinas may have been led to overemphasize humanity's superiority and dominion over nature.[22] But, as we have seen, this right of dominion is balanced against the requirement that human conduct must be in accordance with the ultimate purpose of divine providence. Aquinas could not

[19]Compare with Bryan G. Norton, *Why Preserve Natural Variety*, (Princeton University Press, 1987).

[20]Taylor, 118.

[21]Andrew Linzey, "The Place of Animals in Creation: A Christian View," in *Animal Sacrifices: Religious Perspectives on the Use of Animals in Science*, edited by Tom Regan, (Temple University Press, 1986), 148, note 44.

[22]"Through these considerations we refute the error of those who claim that it is a sin for a man to kill brute animals. For animals are ordered to man's use in the natural course of things, according to divine providence. Consequently, man uses them without any injustice, either by killing them or by employing them in any other way." *Summa Contra Gentiles* 3.112.12.

have imagined the extent to which humanity would achieve an almost total control over nature, and thus, the extent to which this domination could easily come to contradict the very aim of divine providence. In our own time this greater aim requires its due.

Aquinas' attitude toward nature can best be described as a version of nonegalitarian biocentrism.[23] As one might expect, he adopts a mean between the extremes of anthropocentrism (only human beings have value) and egalitarian biocentrism (all beings have equal value). In Thomistic terms, all living beings are good or valuable, but this goodness admits of differences in kind. For Aquinas, the fundamental difference separating the beings of greater value from those of lesser value is the possession of reason and free will, the necessary condition for moral agency. Rational agents are thus permitted to use nonrational beings for the sake of their own preservation. Nevertheless, this use must be in accordance with the ultimate preservation of the natural order. Exactly what this entails would have to be decided by practical reason on a case by case basis. In any event, the dominion which humanity has over nature is not an absolute dominion, but a dominion that is limited and defined by the teleological order of nature and the perfection of the universe as ordained by divine providence.

[23]For a comparable contemporary view, see Louis G. Lombardi, "Inherent Worth, Respect, and Rights," *Environmental Ethics 5*, (1983) 257-270. Response by Paul Taylor, "Are Humans Superior to Animals and Plants?" *Environmental Ethics 6*, (1984), 149-160.

NATURAL LAW, BUSINESS ETHICS, AND THE ENVIRONMENT

Thomas B. Spademan

What does natural law/rights theory have to offer environmental ethics? After pointing out that business activity is responsible for a considerable amount of environmental harm, I argue that part of the difficulty in ascertaining business' environmental responsibilities is in determining the proper relationship between strategic, fiduciary duties managers have to business owners, and broader social duties with which strategic duties often seem in conflict. I then point out that this conflict is structurally similar to a familiar problem in classical natural law theories such as Aquinas', in which it takes the form of potential conflict between natural law and human law. I then offer a theory of the proper relationship between strategic and broader social duties drawing on the idea of a role-differentiated morality as developed by Richard Wasserstrom.

I. INTRODUCTION

Business activity looms large in any list of contributors to environmental harms. It may be the single largest contributor globally, the result, as has long been recognized, of the fact that most environmental harms caused by businesses are economic externalities—costs that are so small as to each individual transactor that although they may add up to very significant social harms over all, they do not figure into individual exchange calculations. Examples of environmental harms that are the result of economic externalies are numerous; we may cite the experiences of many industrial cities, such as Gary, Indiana or Detroit, Michigan, where decades of industrial activity have left an environment in which cancer, chronic respiratory problems, and birth defects are much more common than national averages, and where often enough the industry responsible for the environmental degradation has moved elsewhere to secure cheaper labor, or has simply gone out of business.

There has been disagreement on how to conceptualize potential environmental responsibilities that arise in the course of business, partly as a result of a perceived clash between the strategic duties of managers *qua* managers and duties they may have to the community, or even to the environment itself. On the one extreme, theorists such as Milton Friedman have argued that managers owe only fiduciary duties to owners to make money within the limits of the law.[1] At the same time, there has been a growing willingness to extend the fiduciary duty to other stakeholders (employees, the local community, and customers for example), and to use self-regulation, government regulation, taxation, and tortuous liability to limit or eliminate environmental harms.[2] It is difficult to determine how effective these various strategies have been. In any case, it is theoretically significant that while a weak version of stakeholder theory is in the ascendant at present, it *still* treats the strategic duty to make money as primary, and often as in fundamental opposition to other broader social duties, including duties that might arise in connection with potential environmental harms. While it appears to be the case that corporate environmental awareness has increased over the last few decades, the corporate culture has not yet embraced (and is not likely to embrace) the possibility that environmental concerns may sometimes, perhaps more often than not, trump purely strategic concerns.

In this paper I argue that the perceived clash between strategic and broader social duties arises from a lack of a theory prioritizing them. It is thus one requirement of a natural law approach to specify the relationship between these duties, but such is also a historical strength of natural law theories. Building on Aquinas' theory, and drawing on the idea of a role-differentiated morality developed for professional legal ethics by Richard Wasserstrom (among others), I offer a sketch of a resolution of this apparent conflict, which at least in principle identifies the scope and nature of narrowly strategic as well as broader social duties as they apply to businesses. I then apply it to a particular case in which strategic and environmental concerns clash.

[1]Milton Friedman, "The Social Responsibility of Business is to Increase Its Profits," *New York Times Magazine*, September 13, 1970.

[2]C.f., R. Edward Freeman, "The Politics of Stakeholder Theory," 4 *Business Ethics Quarterly* 409 (1994).

II. THE PROBLEM: ROLE DUTIES AND BROADER SOCIAL DUTIES IN CONFLICT

The apparent clash between strategic and broader social duties in business is a specific example of a problem common in ethics, to which natural law theory has offered several possible solutions. This problem may generically be described as involving conflicts between institutionally generated norms—specifying "role duties"[3] —and what is required of us more generally, apart from our membership in specific institutions. In Aquinas, this problem takes the form of conflicts between the requirements of human law and the requirements of natural law.[4] As citizens or legal subjects (as members of the relevant legal institution), we have a *prima facia* duty to obey human laws, but more or less frequently human laws may come into conflict with natural law. This problem arises in an interestingly new form in business ethics, in which strategic fiduciary duties (to make money for an employer) may come into conflict with broader social duties (not to destroy or harm extensively a shared environment, for example).

Conflicts between institutional role duties and broader social duties may be and have been resolved in various ways. (a) One might assert the absolute primacy of the more general (moral) law; (b) one might assert the absolute primacy of role duties; or (c) one may try to achieve some balance between social and role duties. Option (a) is initially perhaps the most attractive. It is "the moral high road," and Martin Luther King, Jr.

[3]A role duty is a duty one has as a member of an institution, such as a business or the law; the specific duties one has as a member of that institution vary according to the role one plays within it. Thus, for example, a lawyer is often bound by a duty of confidentiality in cases in which a non-lawyer might not be similarly bound. The term is Richard Wasserstrom's; c.f., Richard A. Wasserstrom, "Lawyers as Professionals: Some Moral Issues," *Human Rights*, vol. 5, no. 1, (1975), pp. 1-24.

[4]Aquinas defines natural law as the "participation of the eternal law in the rational creature." *Summa Theologica*, Question 91, Second Article, "Is There a Natural Law in Us?" excerpted in Saint Thomas Aquinas, *On Law, Morality and Politics*, edited by William P. Baumgarth and Richard J. Regan, S.J. (Indianapolis: Hackett Publishing Company, 1988), p. 20. Human law is defined as a set of "particular determinations, devised by human reason…" in *Summa Theologica*, Question 91, Third Article, "Is There a Human Law?" excerpted in Aquinas, *On Law, Morality and Politics*, p. 21.

appealed to it with great rhetorical efficacy in his "Letter From Birmingham Jail." But it is ultimately problematic, not because it seems to require an unerring ability to identify that road (all three possibilities involve similar epistemological difficulties), but because it is insensitive to the benefits of stability that can accrue from common commitment to an imperfect set of institutional rules. Option (b) is likewise problematic, for it requires a kind of institutional loyalty and blindness that seems inconsistent with our rich moral lives. Nonetheless, appeal to it has been and is very common, notoriously in trials for war crimes, in which appeals to role duties are sometimes made in defense of otherwise appalling actions, but also in more subtle ways by various professionals seeking ways out of morally ambiguous situations.[5] In its worst forms it is nothing more than a cult of the institution.

So we are thus, like Aquinas, compelled to embrace option (c).[6] But how shall we determine the proper balance between role duties and social duties? How shall we determine when a given case is one in which we should act from our role duties, or rather a case in which we should act from broader social duties?

To simplify our investigation of this problem, let us narrow the question to consideration of a situation in which the pursuit of strategic goals would produce significant environmental harm such that it might plausibly be said that it violates broader social duties. In the remainder of this paper I propose a model of business environmental ethics that will help us balance social and institutional duties in such a case. I derive this model from the dominant model of legal professional ethics, in which

[5]For example, the U. S. Supreme Court several years ago refused to allow a defense of actual innocence as a constitutional claim, arguing for a very narrow version of their constitutionally defined roles as reviewers of law and not fact. The result was that Leonel Herrera, who had presented evidence of his actual innocence that certainly amounted to reasonable doubt, but not until after the statutory limit on new evidence had run out, was executed, while the court's majority claimed that there was nothing they could do. *Herrera v. Collins*, 506 U.S. 390, 113 S.Ct. 583, 122 L.Ed. 2d 203 (1993). For a discussion of this case and its implications for professional ethics, see my paper "Sartre, Institutional Function, Injustice, and Professional Ethics," in Yeager Hudson, editor, *Technology, Morality and Social Policy* (Lewiston, N. Y.: The Edwin Mellen Press, 1998), pp. 265-283.

[6]In Question 96, Second Article, of the *Summa Theologica*, "Whether it

one's actions are measured in terms of institutionally defined role-duties, but with a crucial limitation: I identify the conditions under which those role duties may be overridden or ignored, tying those role duties to reflective assessment of the purposes and justice of the underlying institution.

III. A CASE STUDY

Consider the following, rather common scenario. You are a manager of a national corporation, which aspires to international status. The manufacturing process of one of your most profitable products produces a moderate amount of toxic waste, which you have treated in accordance with U.S. law, at great expense, with the result that there has been little if any environmental impact. You now have the opportunity to move the manufacturing of this product to a developing country, where the laws governing toxic emissions are much less stringent than U.S. laws. It is clear that such a move would improve the bottom line. It would also result in significant harm to the environment around your plant. You are just a bit uncomfortable with this, but are not sure what to do. Every business instinct tells you to increase profits (after all, it's what you've been hired to do), and you know all the arguments that might be used to justify the move: let the locals take care of themselves, they must know what they are doing, it's their country, you'd only be providing much-needed jobs, and so on. Still, you remain uncomfortable with the thought that you'd be releasing harmful chemicals into the local environment, and it seems to you that the country is willing to make a Faustian bargain.

The problem here is that the manager lacks a principled way to think through the various strategic and social duties, lacks some way of priori-

---

Belongs to Human Law to Repress All Vices?": "Now human law is framed for the multitude of human beings, the majority of whom are not perfect in virtue. Therefore human laws do not forbid all vices, from which the virtuous abstain, but only the more grievous vices, from which it is possible for the majority to abstain; and chiefly those that are injurious to others, without the prohibition of which human society could not be maintained." Saint Thomas Aquinas, *On Law, Morality and Politics*, p. 67. Aquinas seems committed to the principle that when enforcement would cause some unrest, it is acceptable for human law to deviate from the requirements of natural law. Depending on how one interprets "grievous" and by implication what count as "lesser" vices, and the acceptable extent of unrest (mere grumbling, or something more?), the allowable deviation from natural law could be quite great.

tizing them. Should she simply act in accordance with her role duties (move the plant and maximize profits), or should she worry about the potential environmental harms? How should they be balanced? Should they be balanced? Where should she start in her analysis of the situation? Without a way to think through the various competing duties, there is the danger that her decision will be made for bad reasons (e.g., organizational pressure to make money at whatever cost to others), and simply justified after the fact by appeal to arguments of the sort we've noted above.

IV. WHAT'S BUSINESS FOR?

Key to solving the manager's problem is to recall that strategic business duties are only derivatively duties. They have normative force only as a result of our commitment to the institution embodying those norms, in this case, a market form of political economy. In order to prioritize the various duties (strategic or broader social duties), we need first to be clear about the purposes and values of the underlying institution of business. At the same time, we'd like analysis that helps identify the manager's role in the institution, and hence the role duties that apply to her.

Consider for a moment a distinction commonly drawn between public and private law, that is, laws that regulate the relationship between governments and citizens, or between governments (e.g., criminal law, constitutional law), and laws that regulate relationships between individuals, (contract, property, torts, tenancy, employment, e.g.).[7] This distinction is useful in the present context in four ways.

First, the distinction reflects our commitment to certain basic underlying values, and with them a vision of what it means to be a human being, which business as an institution is intended to instantiate: the value

[7]The terms "public" and "private law" are used in several (usually inconsistent) ways, including the following two: (1) to distinguish between laws which regulate government and its relationship to citizens and other governments, and laws which regulate relationships between individuals (the most common definition, sometimes stated in terms of the who or what is the relevant right or duty holder, an individual or a government); and, less commonly, (2) to distinguish law *created* by governments (legislation, common law) and law *created* by individuals (in private contracts, for example). In fact, no definition of either term seems unobjectionable. Although I adopt the first definition, what's important here is not that the distinction works, but that it is relied upon, in an attempt to delineate distinct public and private spheres and hence give institutional expression to the values implied in the distinction.

of autonomous free choice in the form of freedom of contract operating in a private sphere, and the realization of individuality or personality through its objectification in private property. These are the central values of the main areas of private law, contract and property. Additionally, the law is designed to protect us from harm caused by others (tort law), and from government interference in our autonomous pursuit of objectified individuality (property) through free contracts. Protection from unwarranted government intervention in the private sphere is the central theme of criminal and constitutional law (the core areas of public law), and reflects a commitment to an idea of political liberty as (negative) freedom of opportunity to pursue individual goals in the private sphere. All of this is commonplace.

Second, the distinction between public and private law also at least in part structures and instantiates the norms that give rise to business as an institution. There are private law norms as they apply to business (e.g., norms created by contracts), and public law norms as they apply to business (e.g., constitutional and criminal law concerning commercial transactions), which together shape a given business, as a nexus of contracts, constitutional norms, and norms from other areas of law. Hence those norms describe at least in part the roles and role duties of each actor in that institution. (I say "at least in part" because, as I shall argue in a moment, these legal norms can be seen as supplements to a set of analogous moral norms.)

The theoretical distinction between public and private law norms, however, is not put into practice as "cleanly" as theory suggests it should be; there are ways in which what look a lot like public law norms *limit* freedom of contract, including contracts that create forms of business. That is, there are public laws that look to be invasions in the private sphere. OSHA style laws are a familiar example; they are often treated conceptually as public intrusions in the private sphere of contract. How can we explain these departures from the rather simple model at the historical and conceptual basis of our system of political economy?

We can view these as attempts to address injustices or shortcomings in the instantiation of the underlying institution (e.g., OSHA style limitations on freedom of contract are intended to address shortcomings of "pure" freedom of contract as it developed historically), injustices which may arise because the real world doesn't always act as theory says it should (i.e., there are no perfect markets), or because the underlying values instantiated in the institution are themselves unjust. Laws of the OSHA sort are therefore to be distinguished from the core examples of public law, since they are justified not in terms of regulating the relationship between a government and its subjects, but as "correctives" designed to make the world work the way theory says it should. We will call laws of this sort "public laws aimed at institutional defects," as distinct from "public laws proper" and "private laws proper."

Third, the distinction between public and private law is not only useful in identifying the limits and structure of business as an institution, and hence the values it instantiates. The distinction between public and private law suggests a parallel distinction between moral norms that are analogous to private law norms, and moral norms that are analogous to the different kinds of public law norms. On this view, the law in a market democracy is intended as a minimum statement of a more expansive set of moral norms—a sort of consensus "best guess" at the minimum content of the natural law. We can thus use the norms stated in various areas of the law to infer the content of the more expansive moral norms.

An example of a private moral norm might be found in moral duties that arise as a result of the personal relationships that develop in the course of business. These relationships can be seen as giving rise to expectations, and with them moral duties, that are purely the result of a "private moral agreement" (analogous to an actual, legal contract) that arises between the parties. The idea of the "course of business" sometimes recognized in the law as a basis for modification of a contract is a good example of this. If our supposition that the law is best understood as a minimum statement of a more expansive set of moral norms is correct, we can generate a long list of private moral norms simply by analogy to private legal norms. Fair contracting might require not simply avoiding fraud, for example, but a positive determination that the other party understand the terms of the contract.

Examples of public moral norms proper analogous to public law norms are a bit more difficult to find. A public moral norm proper would apply to the parties because of some accepted societal value, perhaps. For example, the moral duty to be truthful, especially when not enforced by a law, can be treated as a public moral norm proper; the law may not prohibit sales puffery, but it is morally a questionable practice. Conceptually, the difference between public and private moral norms parallels the difference between legal duties which we have as a result of some formal agreement or practice (private law norms), and those which we have simply as citizens or legal subjects (public law norms), and, again, a process of analogy with public legal norms should be useful in generating a list of public moral norms.

What might be an example of a public moral norm aimed at institutional defects? It would have to be a moral duty that arises as a result of a defect in or failure of the institutionalization of public and private moral norms proper. One example might be whistle blowing. It often seems justified, and perhaps required, when ordinary moral duties fail, perhaps as a result of organizational pressures that tend to suppress a harmful truth about a product or an activity. In such a case a person with the relevant knowledge may have a duty to blow the whistle.

We can thus construct the following taxonomy of norms, which collectively express the values underlying the institution of business, structure the institution of business, and give rise to the roles, which define managerial duties:

	Legal Norms	**Moral Norms**
Public proper	public law proper (e.g. criminal law)	Moral duties that arise as a result of being members of society (e.g., the ethical extension of the values implied in tort or criminal law.)
Public - aimed at institutional defects in private institutions	laws that limit private law, especially freedom of contract (including biz org., environmental law, parts of contract law, securities law)	Moral duties that arise as a result of a defect in the institutionalization of public moral norms proper (e.g. whistle blowing duties)
Private (individually created)	Private law (contracts, employment, tenancy)	Moral duties that arise as a result of privately created relationships (e.g. the ethical extension of contract law)

The picture that is emerging from our investigation is both simple and powerful, for both ethical analysis and as a basis for understanding the general contours of the law as an attempt to state the minimal ethical commitments of the community. That is, the fourth reason the public/private law distinction, and its extension to moral norms, is useful for business environmental ethics is that it indicates a way of prioritizing the various strategic and broader social norms that are usually implicated in typical environmental business ethics problems. Here's how it seems to work:

> 1. The commitment to the idea of freedom as free, autonomous choice is embodied in the private legal and moral norms concerning (a) the process of contracting, (b) the protection of private property, and (c) the protection from harms caused by other individuals. These areas of the law and ethics are intended to give effect to our liberty interests, protected by public legal and moral norms.
>
> 2. Our liberty interests do not legitimately extend to the harms regulated by the criminal law (harms to the state), or the ethical duties from which they are derived—that is, actions covered by public legal and ethical norms properly so-called.
>
> 3. Because the instantiation of the model in (1) doesn't work quite as it should in theory (e.g., sometimes people are not in equal bargaining positions, or sometimes there arise harms that seem more serious than the correlative limitation on contract), we accept limitations in the form of certain public legal and moral norms "aimed at institutional defects," that is, at defects in the way in which we have institutionalized our commitment to the values of "pure" freedom of contract and private property.
>
> 4. Finally, a given attempt to institutionalize a set of values (the stuff in 1 and 2) may be so flawed, or the values themselves may be so repugnant, that we should give up and start over, if there are either better values or a better way of institutionalizing the accepted values.

(1) and (2) together specify the roles and role-differentiated duties of people in business, while (3) and (4) address problems with the justice of the institution created by the norms in (1) and (2). (3) addresses problems that can be fixed by a little tampering with the rules (reform), and (4) concerns the extreme cases where such reform is not possible, either because (a) there is disagreement about or rejection of the basic societal values (in which case you get a revolution), or (b) where there is no disagreement

about the basic societal values, but the institutions created simply don't work and require wholesale revision.

From this, we can derive a procedure to follow when faced with any potential ethical problem, one which solves our original problem, at least in theory, by prioritizing role and social duties, but with the balance tipped strongly in favor of the underlying social values:

> A. First, what *private moral norms* bear on the action? (e.g., is it a contract? If so, it is subject to the moral duties of fair contracting.)
>
> B. Does the proposed course of action violate any of the *public moral duties*, outlined in (2) above?

(Together, A and B add up to the role-differentiated morality applicable to the person contemplating action.)

> C. Would the moral purposes of the institution be served by the action, that is, would the course of action, even if in accordance with the role-differentiated duties defined in A and B, frustrate the goals of the underlying institution? (For example, would freedom of contract be frustrated in the absence of some legal protection for people who are not really in equal bargaining positions? This may be the way to make sense of the moral duties that OSHA style laws are meant to enforce.) If the form of institutionalization doesn't achieve what it is supposed to achieve, then some "public moral norm aimed at an institutional defect" comes into play, making an otherwise morally acceptable action unacceptable.
>
> D. Finally, is the underlying institution so unjust that even when modified it violates some deeply held human value? For example, suppose that the underlying value of free, autonomous choice were not in fact realized by the law and ethics of contracting and private property, and that no modification along the lines suggested in (C) above would solve the problem. In such a case it would seem that the institutionalization of the value, in contract and property law and ethical norms, should be abandoned. Or suppose that we rejected the value of free autonomous choice, in which case we would probably need to remake our basic political and economic institutions.

V. APPLICATION AND SUMMARY

It is important to note what this account accomplishes, and what it doesn't. It doesn't automatically provide answers in any specific case. Missing is a theory of justice, the foundation on which our political economic institutions are built, and the account stays intentionally agnostic about which theory is correct. We might, for example, reject the idea that a constitutional market democracy effectively realizes autonomous development of personality through objectification, and seek some other political-economic form in which to realize those values, perhaps retaining the democratic element but allowing significant limitations on markets. Or we might reject the values of contractual autonomy, in favor of the maximal development of the potential of a few members of society, or any other of a large set of possible basic values and visions of what it means to be human. In any case, wherever those values are institutionalized in some form of political economy, the process used to think through potential ethical problems will be the same: we must first consider what our role duties are, test a proposed course of action against the purposes of the system, and finally test those purposes against a theory of justice. The benefit here is that the approach requires consideration of justice at the most fundamental level—it does not allow us to simply invoke our role duties and leave it at that. Additionally, the approach provides the manager with an orderly way of working through all of the relevant issues, one which, I think, accurately captures the common phenomenology of such situations; the manager starts with role duties and moves to broader concerns which ultimately may trump those specific role duties.

Incidentally, note as well that this model allows for legal but not moral responsibility for corporations. Essentially, for pragmatic purposes, the fiction of corporate personality may be retained for purposes of legal responsibility, but ultimately the model assigns moral responsibility to individual actors, since it imposes on them the requirement that they make a reasonable assessment not just of their role duties, but of the overall justice of the set of norms institutionalized as well.

Let's return to our case study. We left our manager thinking about various conflicting duties—strategic business duties, duties to others not to harm the environment, possible duties to the environment itself. How might she organize and prioritize these duties given the model we've been developing?

First, she must identify her role within the institution. Here she is a manager, and as a manager her role is to make money, as much as she can consistent with the norms—moral and legal—which structure business and her role within it. The specific duties can be determined by identifying private and public moral norms that apply in this situation—duties to contract fairly with the representatives of the new country, to avoid harm of the sort actionable as a tort (although, again, the requirements of tort law probably don't go far enough in characterizing the harms that might be morally impermissible), to avoid criminal behavior, and so on. Here the potential environmental harm was specified in the hypothetical to be quite significant, and adding some detail might convince her that even if it's legal, it is immoral. The hypothetical is contrary to some public moral norm not to harm others.

But suppose she can't quite decide if the environmental harm is so much as to violate the moral norm analogue of tort law. She then might move on to a consideration of the extent to which the proposed move is consistent with the underlying purposes of the institution. We've identified these as the realization of free autonomous choice through contracts, and the realization of personality through the objectification of self in private property. Here if the environmental harms are great enough, it is clear that future autonomous choice would be limited. And it then becomes important to understand the context of the potential contract: it is not free in the first place, to the extent that the representatives of and workers in the new country are offered only a choice between economic development with significant environmental harm, and no development. The context of the proposed bargain makes it clear that it would not be consistent with the underlying values of autonomous free contract, since the conditions of free contract are absent.

Finally, even if our manager should reject this argument, there are still questions about the fundamental values on which our market democracy is based. Our manager might accept Marxian or feminist critiques of these values, as exploitative, or as patriarchal. Again, on the model developed here, what ultimately counts is the theory of justice and the vision of the human being we choose to institutionalize; these are not questions that should be avoided. As a result, it is not sufficient merely to identify one's role and role duties, although that is a necessary first step. One must deliberately commit oneself to a theory of justice and a vision of human being as well. Although many in business would presently see this requirement as burdensome and academic, this simply indicates to me a flaw in our present corporate culture.

PROCREATION IN THE AGE OF EXTINCTIONS: DOES NATURAL LAW SUPPORT A DUTY TO REDUCE HUMAN POPULATION?

Frank W. Derringh

"Why should we believe that . . . a decrease in human population is obligatory?" asks Max Oelschlaeger in his book, *The Idea of Wilderness*.[1] He was responding to the environmental position known as deep ecology, which defends the intrinsic value of all species and their equal right to a flourishing existence. Oelschlaeger's query is answered here through analysis of a corollary duty to reduce fertility, as the path to population reduction patently preferable to increasing death rates. Because of their political and ideological influence, traditional natural-law considerations militating against (some) population control policies are assessed and refuted by a biologically-based natural law doctrine which strongly supports humanity's obligation to reduce its numbers to save nature.

I. A DUTY TO LOWER FERTILITY RATES

Arguments urging fertility rate reduction to or below replacement levels are not new. Through their I = PAT formula (in which I = environment impact, P = population, A = affluence or consumption level, and T = technology) and emphasis on the need for population reduction, the Ehrlichs have gained notoriety in the eyes of some but also publicity for this issue.[2] Bill McKibben, in his recent opus, *Maybe One*, makes an adroit tactical effort toward the same goal.[3] Others, like Lester Brown of the Worldwatch Institute, have been dubbed "neo-Malthusians"

[1]Max Oelschlaeger, *The Idea of Wilderness* (New Haven: Yale University Press, 1991), p. 306.

[2]For example, Paul R. Ehrlich, Anne H. Ehrlich, and Gretchen C. Daily, *The Stork and the Plow* (New York: Simon & Schuster, Inc., 1991), Paul R. Ehrlich and Anne H. Ehrlich, *Healing the Planet* (New York: Addison-Wesley Publishing Company, Inc., 1991), and Paul R. Ehrlich and Anne H. Ehrlich, *The Population Explosion* (New York: Simon & Schuster, Inc., 1990). Criticism of the "formula" is widespread. See, for example, Martin W. Lewis, *Green Delusions* (Durham: Duke University Press, 1992), p. 238; Philip Sarre and John Blunden, eds.: *An Overcrowded World?* (Oxford: Oxford University Press, 1995), pp. 69-73.

[3]Bill McKibben, *Maybe One* (New York: Simon & Schuster, 1998).

by their opponents for their predictions that widespread famine will erupt soon if humanity does not halt its population explosion.[4]

In order to render their case convincing to Homer Simpson and family, these writers mostly employ what environmental ethicists label an anthropocentric approach. That is, they emphasize the adverse consequences for humanity itself of our not addressing the array of global-health problems exacerbated by overpopulation, including greenhouse gas emissions and subsequent climate change, ozone holes, topsoil degradation and loss, biodiversity reduction, depletion of fish populations, chemical pollution, and so on. Apparently they believe that appeals to nature's own values—its beauty, diversity, integrity, life, and sentience—while perhaps legitimate, are not strong enough to inspire environmentally safer practices.

Nonetheless, these human-centered arguments for fertility reduction are ultimately unsatisfactory. For one thing, so-called neo-Malthusians are accused of exaggerating future perils and present harms to humans from current practices and technology, while overlooking or downplaying the enormous advances in human well-being during the very last fifty years which have witnessed by far the sharpest increase in human population growth rates in history, advances such as considerably longer life spans, increased per-person calorie consumption, phenomenal agricultural gains, and control over many previously deadly diseases. A standoff exists between those who stress the gains from, and those who testify to the costs of, these advances.[5]

More important than this dispute, however, is the ethical quandary posed for humanity by the indisputable fact that the major ramifications of economic growth and multiplying population fall on non-humans. The central question is not why the human species might well find it desirable

[4]Robert Cassen et al., *Population and Development: Old Debates, New Conclusions* (New Brunswick: Transaction Publishers, 1994), p. 24 ("modern Malthusians"), p. 149 ("neo-Malthusians"). Solon L. Barraclough, *An End to Hunger? The Social Origins of Food Strategies* (London: Zed Books Ltd., 1991), p. 210 ("Neo-Malthusian Doctrines"). Georges Sabagh, "Demography and Population Movements," in Richard W. Bulliet, ed., *The Columbia History of the 20th Century* (New York: Columbia University Press, 1998), p. 543 ("neo-Malthusians").

[5]Paul Hawken, Amory Lovins, and L. Hunter Lovins, *Natural Capitalism* (Boston: Little, Brown, and Company, 1999), pp. 309-310.

to slow or to stop or to reverse the momentum that now adds almost 80 million people to the world's population each year,[6] but rather whether humanity is not obligated to do much more than this by, among other steps, reducing fertility as far and as fast as possible by morally acceptable means, because of our responsibility for nature's despoliation.

Doubtless some people will object that humanity does not wrong nature in using it as resources for our benefit. Several reasons are commonly offered to support this claim; for example, humanity's alleged superiority to other organisms. Conversely, some would assert that we are simply doing what (other) animals do, only more effectively. That is, we employ after all our own natural powers to secure our existence and live happily. Comprehensive replies to these and other like-minded theses are not possible here, but even succinct answers require drawing useful distinctions.

Notice that the objection is that the harm done to nature is not wrongful. No one can sensibly deny the widespread human-caused harms to nature—destruction of entire ecosystems; pain, suffering, and death to sentient animals; the stunting of natural tendencies and tropisms in and death of insentient animals and plants; and increasing rates of species' extinctions. But are these *wrongful* harms? The burden of proof, given the state of the world, and the widely appreciated value of life, is surely on humanity to justify its actions, perhaps by reference to the great good thus achieved, allegedly not achievable by other means at a lesser cost to nature, with the harm to nature not having been deliberately aimed at, but rather being the necessary by-product of accomplishing what is good. *Prima facie*, this argument that our ends justify animals' being the means is implausible to environmentalists, since the magnitude of the destruction, and its sources in carelessness, callousness, and myopia (it often harms future people, as well) undermine the appeal to its necessity for

[6]Estimates differ. Lester R. Brown, Michael Renner, and Christopher Flavin, Eds. *Vital Signs 1998* (New York: W.W. Norton & Company, Inc., 1998), p. 102 give an increase of 80 million for 1997. John W. Wright *et al.*, *The New York Times Almanac: 2000* (New York: Penguin, 1999), pp. 482-483, citing the U.S. Bureau of the Census, record the improbably precise figure of 77,321,212 for the 1999 increase, less than the (rounded, one supposes) 1996 figure of 78,633,000. If true, this would mean the increase per year is decreasing in absolute numbers.

human survival and comfort. And even this argument may not be sufficient, for it is consequentialist in form, that is, it judges the moral quality of actions by their results; and it presupposes such greater worth of human beings over other organisms that infliction of pain and death for our benefit is unproblematic. But if we adopt a deontological, that is to say, duty-based, perspective drawn from consideration of the kind of actions sanctioned, it is dubious that the powerful and knowledgeable taking advantage of the vulnerable and helpless can be justified by any beneficial outcomes.[7] One example will illustrate this deontological perspective. United States laws do not permit doctors to experiment non-therapeutically on an adult individual against or without his or her informed consent, even if we could thereby envisage discovering a cure for every known disease afflicting humanity. No amount of good consequences should be allowed to outweigh a patient's right to consent to treatment.[8]

Analogous arguments against human use of nature have been advanced. One distinction that even some anthropocentrists (who locate intrinsic value only in humans) might accept as morally significant is drawn by their near opposites, the biocentrists, such as James Sterba and Paul Taylor, who believe there are no ethically relevant differences among species.[9] This radical position holds that strictly impartial principles are formulable for settling conflicts of interest between humans and other organisms. Probably the least contentious of these principles is a

as well as in percentage terms, *possibly* (things can change) a world-historical turning point. Estimating 90 million are Stanley Warner et al., "Global Population Growth and the Demise of Nature," *Environmental Values* 5 (1996), p. 289, and Joel H. Cohen, *How Many People Can the Earth Support?* (New York: W. W. Norton and Company, 1995), p. 11. Predicting 100 million a year is Thomas W. Merrick, "Population Dynamics in Developing Countries," in Cassen, ed., *Population and Development*, p. 90.

[7]See, for example, Robert E. Goodin, *Protecting the Vulnerable* (Chicago: University of Chicago Press, 1985), pp. 179-188.

[8]Robert J. Levine, "Informed Consent," in Warren T. Reich, ed., *The Ethics of Sex and Genetics* (New York: Simon and Schuster Macmillan, 1998), p. 398.

[9]Paul W. Taylor, *Respect for Nature* (Princeton: Princeton University Press, 1986). James Sterba, "A Biocentrist Strikes Back," *Environmental Ethics* 20 (1998), pp. 361-376; *idem*, "From Biocentric Individualism to Biocentric Pluralism," *Environmental Ethics* 17 (1995), pp. 191-207; idem, "Reconciling Anthropocentric and Nonanthropocentric Environmental Ethics," *Environmental Values* 3 (1994), pp. 229-244.

right of preservation (or survival): the human species can do what is necessary to preserve itself but should not "aggress" (to use Sterba's term) against the basic interests of other species merely in order to advance its own non-basic, also called luxury or trivial, needs (hereafter desires). A principle of self-defense is also advanced by biocentrists, stating that humans are entitled to defend their own lives and other vital (and even non-vital) interests against aggression.[10] Furthermore, one could argue that our possessing some mere desires is basic, oxymoronic as that sounds because a life devoted to satisfying only basic needs would not allow for the immense variety of the experiences that enrich human life. Sterba and Taylor seem aware of this since they assert that in the case of humanity the "basic needs" are of much wider range than those of animals.[11] Unfortunately, in that case the gains to preservation of nature flowing from conformity to other biocentric principles (not discussed here) would be unlikely to occur. Extrapolation from present human destruction of nature, as population increases and goods produced to "satisfy" elastic "needs" expand, entails nature's rapid "demise."[12]

Both the biocentrists' distinction between vital needs and desires, and their principles, relate directly to the issue of fertility reduction and personal responsibility for environmental devastation. *Ab initio*, humanity has had to concentrate most of its efforts on mere survival, and even in today's most affluent world approximately a billion people live in so-

[10]Although Sterba does not mention it, the appeal to rights (or even duties) of self-defense and self-preservation forms the basis of the "modern" theory of natural law, initiated by Hugo Grotius to refute revived moral relativism (or skepticism). See Hugo Grotius, *The Law of War and Peace*, tr. Louise R. Loomis (Roslyn, NY: Walter J. Black, Inc., 1949), p. 4, and Richard Tuck, "The 'Modern' Theory of Natural Law," in Anthony Pagden, ed., *The Language of Political Theory in Early-Modern Europe* (Cambridge: Cambridge University Press, 1990), pp. 99-119.

[11]Sterba, "A Biocentrist Strikes Back," p. 365. Taylor, *Respect for Nature*, pp. 281-282. See also Sterba, *Contemporary Social and Political Philosophy* (Belmont, CA: Wadsworth, 1995), pp. 15-19, where "self-development" counts as a "basic need." Also see John Passmore, *Man's Responsibility for Nature*, 2nd ed. (London: Duckworth, 1980), p. 113, which refers to "fundamental human needs" yet, equates their satisfaction with "civilization."

[12]Warner, "Global Population Growth and the Demise of Nature," pp. 285-303.

called "absolute poverty."[13] Only recently has humanity devoted so much intelligence and labor to satisfying, for more than the smallest fraction of the population, what by any definition of "basic needs" would have to be labeled desires—desires for faster automobiles, higher-resolution television screens, and larger houses. In crossing this line on a massive scale, humanity thereby has incurred substantial responsibilities, both to the billion people in destitution and to the pillaged habitats, tortured animals, and species threatened with extinction. In that case, the biocentrists' additional principle of rectification for wrongs committed must come into play.[14]

This moral side of the dilemma in which humanity now finds itself emerged from the saga of human expansion across the globe, extermination of many indigenous species, technological "progress," in short, our story.[15] Only by appreciating this collective narrative can we assume voluntarily and knowingly our responsibility. Only thus will we find the proper path to planetary restoration, reparation, and rectification. True, one person alone does not burn down a forest, but each person contributes to its use for farming or for grazing, creating demand-pressure as, say, an affluent cheeseburger consumer. All are implicated by each. Each constitutes all. This holds both for cause and for consequence, for how we got where we are and how we get from where we are.

Fear of collective responsibility is understandable. No one wants to be blamed for others' misdeeds. Yet we also take pride in our family's,

[13]Again, estimates vary widely. Paul R. Ehrlich and Anne H. Ehrlich, *Betrayal of Science and Reason* (Washington, D.C.: Island Press, 1998), p. 76, estimate 700 million to 1 billion (also see endnote 70, p. 269, for varying estimates from different organizations). Phillips Foster, *The World Food Problem* (London: Adamantine Press, Ltd., 1992), p. xv, estimates that there are well over one billion hungry and undernourished people in the world. Evans claims chronic malnutrition is decreasing in developing countries, both as a percentage and in absolute numbers. L. T. Evans, *Feeding the Ten Billion: Plants and Population Growth* (Cambridge: Cambridge University Press, 1998), p. 187 (figure 28).

[14]Sterba, "A Biocentrist Strikes Back," p. 368. Taylor, *Respect for Nature*, pp. 304-307.

[15]Many debates rage over interpreting this history. Consult: Alfred W. Crosby, *Ecological Imperialism: The Biological Expansion of Europe, 900—1900* (Cambridge: Cambridge University Press, 1986); Clive Ponting, *A Green History of the World* (New York: St. Martin's Press, 1991); Evans, *Feeding the Ten Billion*; and Andrew Goudie, *The Human Impact on the Natural Environment*, 3rd ed. (Cambridge, MA: The MIT Press, 1990).

country's, religion's, or profession's achievements, even if our particular contribution to them was negligible or nonexistent (indeed perhaps more so then). When people exhibit satisfaction at human accomplishments not their own, and possibly at the expense of other living beings, they are witlessly testifying to an identification that does not come ethically cost-free.

The goal of allocations of responsibility, however, is not coarse finger-pointing but stimulating improvements in practices, attitudes, sensibilities, and ruminations. Central to these is realizing how identification of any individual with the traits of the collective human species is self-glorification if not accepting of the tragic and brutal human adventure. This is well illustrated by anthropocentrists when they assert human superiority over animals on the basis of, say, intelligence, yet also claim that even anencephalic individuals, lacking that intelligence while still enjoying the same status as human, are due consideration equal to that extended to all other people, but greatly in excess of that extended to intelligent animals. This much-commented-upon inconsistency, the so-called "marginal cases argument," betrays how we identify ourselves with collective entities for self-serving purposes. Swayed by essentialist thinking, we have allowed our partial identity as humans to overshadow two broader identities: those of living being and planetary resident. We can hardly identify ourselves as integrally human and yet deny that the human history leading to present environmental catastrophes reveals who we are. Crudely put, what they did and are doing manifests, at the very least, potentialities of mine. Additionally, to the extent that I benefit from it without attempting to stop it, I become even more complicit in it.[16] But when each of us acknowledges that human history is *my* history as well as our history, then an obligation, not just a desire, to preserve nature might be recognized. We would then be reintegrating our species-identity into the still larger context of planetary resident.[17]

[16]Analyzing responsibility usefully is Ronnie Z. Hawkins, "Intergroup Justice: Taking Responsibility for Intraspecific and Interspecific Oppressions," *Ethics and the Environment* 3 (1998), pp. 1-40.

[17]For related, but not identical, "self-identity" considerations see Jon Wetlesen, "The Moral Status of Beings who are not Persons: A Casuistic Argument," *Environmental Values* 8 (1999), especially pp. 309-312.

Perhaps it will be said that few of the world's six billion human inhabitants possess sufficient knowledge of the repercussions of their acts for them to be held personally responsible. However, such knowledge is far more common today than before, robbing this contention of some of its force. Additionally, even the most ignorant and illiterate person has some built-in empathy for life and its afflictions.[18] Discounting pain we bring on animals because they *are* animals may be a necessary ploy to avoid or to assuage guilt for taking life in order that we might live.[19] So, while it is indeed true that Everyman's awareness of the full extent of the appalling ramifications for nature of human activities is lamentably limited, this is not an exoneration, given that countervailing, largely selfish motivations inhibit us from acknowledging our emotional responses to pain inflicted and deflect us from acquiring greater knowledge of what we do, information certainly available to many of us.

On the individual level, responsibilities must be differentiated. Some philosophers remind us that in many less "developed" countries poorer people are highly restricted in their options by class oppression, corporate power, the police, and political and military authorities. For these indigent and desperate people to be faulted for seizing part of tropical rainforests is, they say, abominable: it is blaming the victims.[20] Certainly there is much truth in this. But it is condescending to characterize people as *mere* victims and as the passive raw material for exploitation by the powerful and wealthy. Even constrained and coerced decisions *are* choices and have their sequelae.

Given the imminence of nature's "demise," humanity now faces a fateful choice: either to continue understanding ourselves as simultaneously "superior" to nature and yet its destroyer (surely inherently incoherent ideas), or to reconnect with nature's intrinsic values and thus initi-

[18]Peter H. Kahn, Jr., *The Human Relationship with Nature* (Cambridge, MA: MIT Press, 1999). Rod Preece and Lorna Chamberlain, *Animal Welfare and Human Values* (Waterloo, Canada: Wilfred Laurier University Press, 1993). Edward O. Wilson, *Biophilia* (Cambridge, MA: Harvard University Press, 1984).

[19]Walter Burkert, *Homo Necans*, tr. Peter Bing (Los Angeles: University of California Press, 1983).

[20]Andrew Brennan, "Poverty, Puritanism and Environmental Conflict," *Environmental Values* 7 (1998), pp. 305-331. William Aiken, "Ethical Issues in Agriculture," in Tom Regan, ed., *Earthbound* (Prospect Heights, IL: Waveland Press, Inc., 1984), p. 275.

ate a process for locating a non-fatal place on the planet for ourselves. Each family, as a family, will be crucial to this process.

That rapid growth in human numbers is a considerable cause of natural destruction, although contested by a few, is accepted by many scholars.[21] A palpable logic links numbers and the need to supply additional food, housing, jobs, energy, sanitation, education, health care, heating, transportation, clothing, and generally the physical equipment to preserve life. Indisputably other causes contribute to the extirpation of nature, especially modern technology, but also rising living standards and a consumer mentality, inept policy decisions, dictatorial regimes, warfare, anthropocentric human attitudes, wealth inequalities, profit-seeking corporations and their investors: the causes are many, complex, and interconnected. But the numbers also matter; and having passed six billion, they are going to matter even more in the next century.

Why? Because given population momentum due primarily to declining death rates, especially for infants, from improved sanitation, diets, and disease control, a high proportion of the population in underdeveloped countries (45 % in the "least developed" countries) is under the age of 15.[22] Considerable knowledge about *how* to lower fertility rates has been gained, although there is not a single "formula" effective for all peoples, if only because their own wishes must play a crucial role, and these vary greatly.[23]

[21]See books cited in notes 2, 3, 4, 5, 6, 8, 13, 15 above. Also informative (among many others) are: Robert Repetto, ed., *The Global Possible* (New Haven: Yale University Press, 1985); Amartya Sen, *Development as Freedom* (New York: Alfred A. Knopf, 1999); Tim Dyson, *Population and Food: Global Trends and Future Prospects* (New York: Routledge, 1996); Kerstin Lindahl-Kiessling and Hans Landberg, eds., *Population, Economic Development, and the Environment* (Oxford: Oxford University Press, 1994); Lester R. Brown et al., eds., *State of the World 2000* (New York: W. W. Norton and Company, 2000).

[22]Wright, ed., *The New York Times Almanac 2000*, p. 483, citing UN figures for 1996. In "less developed countries" the percentage is 35, while it is 19 in the "more developed countries," and 32 for the world.

[23]Cohen, *How Many People Can the Earth Support?*, p. 371, lists six major factors: ". . .promoting contraceptives; developing economies; saving children; empowering women; educating men; and doing everything at once." However, Cohen writes, p. 370, ". . .no one knows exactly what will work across the whole range of population problems . . ." "Exactly" offers reason for hope; we know the basics.

Granted knowledge of the means to discharge it, a duty to reduce fertility is implied by previously mentioned (although disputable) ethical principles: collective human responsibility for the growing environmental apocalypse; the human tendency to sacrifice others' basic needs to their own desires; the duty to preserve and restore nature; the obligation of non-maleficence to the sentient; the injustice of benefiting from wrongfully inflicted harm; and the nobler ideal of being a member of the planetary community rather than "conqueror" of it.[24]

Given the almost inseparable interconnections between population size and other factors in causing environmental despoliation, how crucial are the decisions for parenting and limiting family size to below replacement level to the task of ending or, more immediately, drastically curtailing, humanity's destruction of nature?

First, for most people, perhaps only excepting those holding substantial political and economic power, no other common life-decision will have as much impact on our environment. In affluent nations every additional person is an enormous drain on natural resources.[25] There can be little doubt that a smaller affluent population, especially if it could ever adopt a more modest or "graceful" lifestyle (not at present very likely), would benefit the natural world.[26] In poorer countries, additional people place further burdens on nature both as their living standards rise, and as the most indigent, whether as pawns of the power-holders, or out of sheer desperation for fuel and food, strip soil of its protective vegetation, attempt to bring marginal land into cultivation, and over hunt wild animals (many forests worldwide are losing all their mammalian life).

A crude argument advanced by Julian Simon provides the grounds for a second perspective on humanity's obligation to restrict its fertility. Any birth, we can infer, might produce another Einstein or, one supposes, Henry Ford. Humans are not only resources for economic growth but also creative beings.[27] Patently, it is equally likely that the next child will be another Pol Pot or Adolf Hitler. Guessing which is more likely—

[24]Aldo Leopold, *A Sand County Almanac and Sketches Here and There* (New York: Oxford University Press, 1949), p. 204.

[25]For criticism of this way of thinking, see Lewis, *Green Delusions*, p. 239.

[26]Jerome M. Segal, *Graceful Simplicity* (New York: Henry Holt, 1999).

[27]Julian Simon in Norman Myers and Julian Simon, *Scarcity or Abundance?* (New York: W.W. Norton & Company, Inc., 1994), p. 33.

Stravinsky or Stalin—hardly conduces to solemn decision-making. But a profounder consideration is hidden here. If people follow Simon's advice they will be creating conditions for inevitable disaster on our finite planet. The number of people, as such, makes a substantial difference to the likelihood that lives of greater value to their possessors, to other people, and to nature itself will be lived. Greater numbers, more cities, more overcrowding—with more need for food and for everything else—are surely disharmonious to finer aspirations. Scale, balance, proportion, community seem key terms, however vague, with which to express what leads to a fulfilling human life.[28] While there are not necessary connections among urban gigantism, inequalities, oppression, envy, *anomie*, warfare, and natural destruction, certainly there seems some reason to believe that optimal living conditions for humans and between humans and nature are found rather in smaller communities involving frequent face-to-face contact, less social stratification, democratic decision-making, and a perceived match between microcosm and macrocosm. If such localized living is to be more than an anarchist's dream, reduced population will be mandatory.[29]

Third, no other massive die-out, such as now appears to be under way, was caused by the success of one species (or indeed any group of species) in monopolizing so much of the planet's resources. For the first time in Earth's history, one species has achieved such hegemony over the planet that it appropriates about 40% of the world's net primary production on land (by certain measurements) with fatal results for many other life forms.[30] Surely this unparalleled development poses a responsibility

[28]Relating considerations of "scale" to how people should treat their surroundings is Bill McKibben, *The End of Nature* (New York: Random House, 1989). Likewise Lewis, *Green Delusions*, pp. 82-116.

[29]The above paragraph contains sweeping, undefended assertions and generalizations, and counterexamples are easy to cite. Like Greek *poleis*, Italian city-states of the late Middle Ages and Renaissance were notoriously bellicose. Environmental advantages accrue to megalopolises given *current* technology and population numbers and distribution (fewer people in rural areas to despoil the environment). National governments are sometimes required to overrule local *indifference* to practices harmful to their own, not to mention others', surroundings. Lewis, n. 28 *supra*.

[30]Ehrlich, Ehrlich, and Daily, *The Stork and the Plow*, p. 170, and Paul R. Ehrlich, "The Loss of Diversity," in E. O. Wilson, ed., *Biodiversity* (Washington, D.C.: National Academy Press, 1988), p. 23.

for all people. Is it even coherent to consider such appropriation justified to further our (alleged) flourishing in the light of our close kinship to other species, not to mention their intrinsically equal need to flourish? It is difficult to reconcile sacralizing *our* life, making its ritualistic invocation in a variety of intrahuman dilemmas almost routine, with our failure to perceive that it is wrong to harm *life*. Furthermore, extinction, by its finality (as so often noted), surely possesses a unique pathos. To cause it is thus correspondingly abominable. Decisions by families which reduce average fertility, and to that extent alleviate pressure on ecosystems, help to change humanity's role from exterminator to preserver, thus honoring the bond of life among members of the planetary community.

One retort to the argument of this paper is that to assert an obligation to reduce fertility is to demand the impossible, especially from busy families enmeshed in the exigent responsibilities of day-to-day life. Even among the ecologically educated, personal and sentimental factors will far outweigh such hypothetical, cerebral considerations.[31] The obvious rebuttal is that a fertility-reduction obligation doesn't require families to have no children, just a number below replacement level. Why should an attempt to link such a decision to its largest ethical context be doomed to futility? Surely it is myopic not to care what the world in which these children will also have children will be like? People in the past probably did not consider this because they expected that, whatever *they* did, the world would stay much the same.[32] No one believes this now. In today's novel circumstances far more is clearly required. Preparation for birth, equally with Plato's preparation for death, must become an examined, a philosophical decision.

[31] See Roger McGinn, "Technology, Demography, and the Anachronism of Traditional Rights," in Merton E. Winston and Ralph D. Edelbach, Eds. *Society, Ethics, and Technology* (Belmont, CA: Wadsworth, 2000), pp. 132-133: "To think that any such possibility [to " . . . cut the rate of increase in the number of rights holders . . . "] could be achieved is utopian at this juncture in Western cultural history." "Utopian"? Why? Population decline is expected in Western Europe over the next 25 years. (Wright, ed., *The New York Times Almanac 2000*, p. 484). A decline from about 729 million to 701 million is projected.

[32] So says historian J. M. Roberts, *Twentieth Century* (New York: Viking, 1999), p.29.

II. NATURAL LAW AND POPULATION

The necessity to stabilize and perhaps reduce human population is widely recognized, albeit for diverse reasons, not only by ecophilosophers but also and increasingly by politicians, citizens, biologists, and, but least of all, economists.[33] Yet the governmental resources devoted to doing so are exiguous.[34] Among the reasons for this, the political and economic clout of some religious groups is not insignificant. The opposition of Roman Catholicism and Islam, religions of about one-third of all people, to fertility control by contemporary technological means is well known.[35] Even when the practices of the faithful diverge from theological tenets (as they frequently do), governments are often fearful of antagonizing them.[36] (The predominantly Protestant U.S.A. is an obvious example.) Natural law is important in Catholic doctrinal reasoning,[37] and is also famously invoked in our nation's most formative political document (with enduring consequences).[38] Furthermore, the views articulated by natural law theorists concerning procreation probably have resonance beyond the religions that explicitly espouse them. So it is practically important for environmentalists to avail themselves of this discourse to advocate fertility-reduction, as long as the medium does not distort the message. It is even possible that one version of natural law might be "true"!

[33]The U.N. Conferences on Population (1974, 1984, and 1994) provide sufficient evidence for this statement. In particular, the shift in position of the "developing" nations (i.e., of their "leaders") between conferences provides noteworthy testimony to their mounting concern about population issues. See Kaval Gulhati and Lisa M. Bates, "Developing Countries and the International Population Debate: Politics and Pragmatism," in Cassen, ed., *Population and Development*, pp. 47-77.

[34]Brown, *Vital Signs* 1998, p. 102.

[35]Islam's traditions and thinkers are divided about the legitimacy of (various forms of) fertility control. John L. Esposito, "Islamic Perspectives," in Reich, ed., *The Ethics of Sex and Genetics*, pp. 510-515.

[36]Ronald M. Green, "Religious Traditions," in Reich, ed., *The Ethics of Sex and Genetics*, p. 510.

[37]Russell Hittinger, "Natural Law," in Reich, ed., *The Ethics of Sex and Genetics*, pp. 485-486.

[38]Garry Wills, *Inventing America: Jefferson's Declaration of Independence* (Garden City, NY: Doubleday and Company, Inc., 1978), especially pp. 186-187.

Natural law is notoriously an expression with almost as many meanings as interpreters.[39] In its most defensible version(s) it understands ethics as an outgrowth of mankind's species' propensities and situation.[40] (Here the salient contrast for "natural" in "natural law" is "conventional:" ethics as merely an artifact of a particular society's broadest self-appraising powers.) Certain functions, objects, events, and processes are conducive to (i.e., good for) the flourishing of, i.e., the realization and development of powers in, humanity (as with *other* species). Humanity is thus understood to constitute a natural kind, possessing a set of virtually universal proclivities and capacities.[41] Among these is the exercise of practical reasonableness, a weighing of alternatives for action, which can be (morally) judged by their adaptiveness to the fulfillment of desires, some of which have evolved to facilitate survival on Earth, others of which lend meaning to our lives by reflecting values discovered in the natural world.[42] Because action answers indeterminacy in *particular* situations and societies (in which universal goods are expressed in manifestly contrasting manners), general natural-law precepts require supplementation by context-dependent thinking (as the ensuing discussion illustrates). Natural law implies, and history corroborates, that ethical rules founder (fail to motivate action) when they violate humanity's deepest attachments and aspirations. Among these bonds, environmental philosophers argue, is Wordsworth's "primal sympathy",[43] comprising a responsive-

[39]Hittinger, "Natural Law," p. 482. Paul Foriers and Chaim Perelman, "Natural Law and Natural Rights," in Philip P. Wiener, ed., *Dictionary of the History of Ideas*, vol. 3, pp. 13-27, claim there are " . . . 120 possible combinations" of meanings of the two words and " . . .almost as many definitions of the expression 'natural law'" (p. 14).

[40]What follows is much indebted to Larry Arnhart, *Darwinian Natural Right: The Biological Ethics of Human Nature* (Albany, NY: State University of New York Press, 1998).

[41]For three discussions of this much-contested claim, see Stephen R. L. Clark, "Is Humanity a Natural Kind?" in Clark, *The Political Animal* (New York: Routledge, 1999), pp. 40-58; Timothy Chappell, "How to Base Ethics on Biology," in T. D. J. Chappell, ed., *The Philosophy of the Environment* (Edinburgh: Edinburgh University Press, 1997), pp. 102-116; Arnhart, *Darwinian Natural Right*, pp. 231-248.

[42]Emphasizing practical reasonableness is John Finnis, *Natural Law and Natural Rights* (Oxford: Clarendon Press, 1980), pp. 100-133.

[43]William Wordsworth, "Intimations of Immortality from Recollections of Early Childhood," quoted in Rod Preece, *Animals and Nature: Cultural Myths, Cultural*

ness to and empathy with life, sensitivity to nature's beauty, subliminal as well as (often) conscious kinship with other organisms, and an awareness, however dimmed by drudgery and civilization, that a shared planetary origin and destiny join humans to other life forms in a symbiosis so profound that our lives become progressively more barren as theirs are ended or stunted. Thus, converting acknowledgment of all species' similar intrinsic value and our "primal sympathy" into the basis for defensible "arguments" the conclusions of which initiate (right) action, i.e., action that allows as far as possible for the unfolding of all beings' natural powers, is one of ecophilosophy's (seemingly) impossible tasks. This version of natural law might be dubbed biological or Darwinian (but it avoids "selfish gene" reductionism)[44], to contrast it with Stoic, Christian, and "modern" (collectively, "traditional") natural law doctrines that lack (or reject) most of the insights provided by evolutionary biology. In traditional natural law, actions are judged morally right when they " . . . promote the values specified by the natural inclinations of human beings."[45] Among these are life and procreation, knowledge and sociability,[46] but Finnis, a contemporary natural-law theorist, lists more.

Traditional natural law thinking about procreation includes the following theses (among others). (1) Couples have a duty, when they engage in sexual congress, to aim at producing children for whom they (or society?) can adequately care.[47] (2) Therefore, humans have a right not to be deprived, and a duty not to deprive themselves, of their procreative capac-

Realities (Vancouver, Canada: UBC Press, 1999), p. 70.

44R. Dawkins, *The Selfish Gene*, new ed. (New York: Oxford University Press, 1989).

45C. E. Harris, Jr., *Applying Moral Theories*, 3rd ed. (Belmont, CA: Wadsworth, 1997), p. 100. "Specified" isn't quite right here. (Inclinations don't "specify" anything.)

46Harris, Jr., *Applying Moral Theories*, p. 101. The former pair he calls "biological values." But Finnis, surely correctly, argues that those values (also?) have cultural and mental dimensions. See further comments in this essay.

47J. Bryan Hehir, "Roman Catholic Perspectives," in Reich, ed., *The Ethics of Sex and Genetics*, pp. 519-520. On a duty (for most) of marriage, Samuel Pufendorf (a major, "modern" natural-law theorist), *On the Duty of Man and Citizen According to Natural Law*, ed. James Tully, tr. Michael Silverthorne (Cambridge: Cambridge University Press, 1991), pp. 120-121.

ity.[48] (3) Sterilization and "artificial" contraception are thus wrong.[49] (4) A human being is a rational creature with "free will" to whose good life nature contributes, but in a purely instrumental way. (5) Prudence or practical wisdom can successfully extrapolate from (or within) natural-law precepts to solve issues arising from massive population growth and "resource" depletion. It need not rely on ecocentric doctrines, which find intrinsic value in the natural environment, and which, it will be asserted, deny the uniqueness of human nature upon which a correspondingly unique human way of life is based, sanctioned, and even sanctified (e.g., marriage as a sacrament). Advancing social justice will solve these issues to the greatest extent morally possible.[50]

These views will strike many environmentalists as both repugnant and ineffectual. They exhibit indifference to the effects of human actions on nature and are complacently anthropocentric in outlook. While promoting social and economic justice should constitute a vital part of a program to reduce fertility, couples also require the *means* to prevent unwanted pregnancies. Social justice cannot do that alone! Only a very profound "interest" deserving adamantine protection could underpin such "rights" and "duties."

The interest often invoked by natural-law theorists is, of course, the deeply felt tie between parents and children, with its enormous social ramifications. Surely this tie explains why some people are disturbed by proposals such as those for parenting licenses.[51] (Opposition to government intervention in intimate matters would be a related, barely distinguishable objection.) This procreative desire is nearly universal, a fact of great significance to many natural law authors, especially Grotius.[52] For him, universality signified "naturalness," a human desire that society and (positive) law must regulate (as all cultures do) in order to adapt it to changing circumstances. Surely the desire to procreate is almost as natur-

[48]Finnis, *Natural Law and Natural Rights*, p. 225.

[49]Harris, Jr., *Applying Moral Theories*, p. 101.

[50]Hehir, "Roman Catholic Perspectives," pp. 518-519.

[51]As mentioned by Professor John J. Conley at the Pace University Conference on "The Ethics of Parenting: New Beginnings," February 25, 1999 (at which an earlier version of this paper was presented).

[52]Grotius, *Law of War and Peace*, pp. 13, 22.

al (universal) as the desire to live. If this isn't "natural" to humanity, what is? Thus, many people might find assertions of a right protecting this desire from (presumably wrongful) societal intrusion "self-evident" (a key claim in the natural law thinking of Aquinas, Grotius, and Finnis, for example). After all, this is not a "right" to be drugged-out, avoid military service, or practice prostitution. On the contrary (it might be claimed), this is a culturally-invariant drive, in the service of species survival, from which, and only from which, broader ties can be forged in the thus affectionately-bonded offspring.[53]

However, objections to a natural-law prohibition on contraceptive use remain. Why should all sexually active couples *always* aim at procreation? Can't they aim at pleasure within a loving relationship? Can't they prevent conception to have more time to pursue truth, as scientists or poets? Can't they believe a greater quality of life will come to existing children by preventing further births?[54] Additionally, isn't the largest ethical context of procreative decision-making, i.e., effects of human acts on nature, relevant at all? Isn't the possibility that long-term human survival might be endangered by overpopulation (and actions harmful to the planet) germane to the practical rationality of decisions for parenting?

To answer these kinds of questions, natural-law theorists deploy a formidable armamentarium. Some theorists infer from a "natural inclination" to engage in sexual intercourse a "negative" duty against contraceptive use.[55] But seeking pleasure seems just as "natural." (Nozick's "experience machine" does not prove otherwise.[56] It only "proves," at most, that pleasure is not our only good.) Much more important, however, is that natural-law thinkers themselves do not contend that copulating on impulse is a human value, i.e., a value for or of a being with delibera-

[53]Arnhart, *Darwinian Natural Right*, pp. 89-121, 211-230.

[54]These reasons for preventing procreation at all, or limiting the number of one's offspring, appeal to values natural-law theorists do or might recognize as "universal" goods for humanity. Harris, Jr., *Applying Moral Theories*, pp. 101-110.

[55]Harris, Jr., *Applying Moral Theories*, p. 101.

[56]As Harris seems to believe. Supra, p. 110. Robert Nozick, *Anarchy, State, and Utopia* (New York: Basic Books, 1974), pp. 42-45. In this machine you would experience bliss, but never be able to *act*.

tive reason.[57] Sex for a human being is not the same as sex for a dog. This contention, however, cuts against the ban on contraceptives. It is sufficient to refute the notion that condoms are "artificial" and hence their use wrong. Inventiveness is as much a human value as knowledge, of which indeed it is a type (know-how). Once it is granted that humans can contemplate the point and purpose of their deeds, the *mere* desirability of sexual intercourse is quite insufficient to ground a universal duty against frustrating its (possible) outcome.[58]

Natural law theorists also argue that the use of contraceptives is "directly" against the value of procreation. Natural-law thinkers assert that one should never, directly, "violate" or "devalue" a basic human value.[59] Thus, according to the double-effect doctrine, one is not allowed to cause an evil if the evil is the means of bringing about a good. Aiming at the good of a higher quality of life for one's children by preventing further offspring does just that (natural-law thinkers assert). But this argument begs the question, by assuming that some harm has been done or value "infringed." What harm? Which value? Certainly the *instrumental* (and objective) good of procreation has not been frustrated, i.e., species survival. This goal does not require for its attainment that every couple intend children with every sexual act; it may, in fact, require fewer births. Nor is its *intrinsic* good "violated." For *whom* is this good intrinsic? Only for those who wish children. Surely natural law does not imply because most couples want children, you must also? This grotesque (mis-) interpretation would render it unworthy of discussion.

Aquinas attempts to draw a distinction between the "accidental" and essential features of an ethical situation. "[N]atural rectitude in human acts is not dependent on things accidentally possible in the case of one individual, but, rather, on the conditions which accompany the entire

[57]This retort builds on Aristotle's observation that the rational soul influences the functioning of the sensitive and nutritive souls. Finnis replies to Singer's "reliance on sentience" moral criterion by invoking this retort in his *Natural Law and Natural Rights*, pp. 194-195.

[58]But this conjures up the enormous difficulty of how correctly to "extrapolate" obligations from natural desires, which rule out certain ethical principles as impractical, thus bolstering the "ought implies can" dictum.

[59]"Violate" is the odd term of Harris, Jr., *Applying Moral Theories*, p. 103. "Devaluation" is the term of Finnis, *Natural Law and Natural Rights*, p. 105.

species."[60] On this basis, he reasons that husband and wife should remain together after their child's birth even should the wife be able to care for the child alone. The latter is the "accidentally possible" circumstance. But on what basis is this less "essential" than the man's "right" to rule the roost? Wouldn't the surely most "essential" ethical feature of the situation—the child's welfare—be better upheld sometimes if the child remained with the mother? Aquinas' distinction seems even more unhelpful when procreation in the age of extinction is concerned. To dismiss massive natural harms as "accidents" with no relevance to procreative rights is tantamount to claiming a "right" to do wrong![61] It is also "self-refuting," since as natural beings we need to honor our Earth to deserve any imputed "self-respect." Furthermore, the duty of restitution, previously mentioned, must also be acknowledged as relevant to humanity's future choices.

A more promising Catholic natural-law theme is the empowerment of women as an essential constituent of social justice. Such empowerment can be interpreted as an extension of the central role of practical rationality in many natural-law doctrines since Aristotle, which emphasize the significance to a good life of viewing one's life as a whole.[62] A good life requires "planning" or pondering, in order to weave present actions into a meaningful pattern of judiciously assessed events and encounters. Existing limitations in many nations on women's participation in domestic as well as political democracy, education, and employment are not conducive to the exercise of this agency-freedom which natural law respects and requires.[63] Consequently, arguments from the "unnaturalness" of contraceptive technology are not only refutable as above but as part of a larger natural-law case for the role of deliberative reason in fulfilling life goals, and indeed in being able to set them for oneself in the first place.

[60]From Aquinas, *Summa Contra Gentiles*, Book Three, quoted in Anne Minas, ed., *Gender Basics*, 2nd ed. (Belmont, CA: Wadsworth Publishing Company, 2000), p. 393.

[61]Hittinger, "Natural Law," p. 487.

[62]Julia Annas, *The Morality of Happiness* (Oxford: Oxford University Press, 1993), pp. 27-46. Rawls and Finnis also stress this idea.

[63]Sen argues for the centrality of incorporating respect for agency-good into "development" schemes in his *Development as Freedom*.

If the argument thus far advanced is cogent, no plausible natural-law reason exists to oppose informed and voluntary use of medically safe contraceptive devices to limit family size, and some reasons exist to support their use. Would, however, coercion be justifiable in order to reduce fertility? Still more difficult questions are at what level should humanity stabilize its population? How should that level be determined? Most fundamentally: are we lowering population for our benefit or that of nature?

Environmentalists often claim that coercive fertility reduction is ineffective in anything but the very short-term. It generates resentment that makes it more difficult to obtain voluntary cooperation when coercion ceases. Furthermore, the broadly social, domestic, and economic measures that encourage fertility decline are beneficial (from most points of view) to parents, children, and society; they thus have correspondingly more to be said for them.[64] Furthermore, given the assumption that freedom as such is a good—and that it is restrictions on it that require justification—a heavy burden of proof rests on proponents of coercion, especially given the invasive nature of reproductive coercion. This argument again points to a pervasive feature of the human condition—agency goodness or "autonomy"—to ground a moral presumption. This is a natural-law kind of appeal and perhaps the most popular type in Anglo-American philosophy.[65]

Nonetheless, invocation of very general (alleged) features of the "human predicament" to rule out coercion is unsatisfactory. Too much value can be placed on "autonomy," its very reality is questionable, and its centrality in social policy sometimes has dire results.[66] Additionally, as Amartya Sen points out, what counts as a "need" can be relative to available information about what is "feasible."[67] It might already be true that human despoliation of the environment has reached such proportions that catastrophe for both humanity and other organisms is imminent (indeed,

[64]Sen, *Development as Freedom*, pp. 204-226.

[65]Hittinger, "Natural Law," pp. 484-485.

[66]Willard Gaylin and Bruce Jennings, *The Perversion of Autonomy* (New York: The Free Press, 1996).

[67]Sen, *Development as Freedom*, p. 154.

already occurring). If authoritarianism could be trusted to ameliorate the situation, some might (and do) find that a desirable option.[68]

However, there is little, if any evidence that tyranny could be trusted. That tyrants try to prolong their stay in power at great social cost is obvious. More acceptable would be democratic governments supporting "coercive" (i.e., legislated) measures *directly* influencing fertility choices, e.g., financial penalties on some families (depending on income) with more than, say, two children, or/and bonuses for those with fewer. Given present attitudes in the U.S.A, at least, this kind of policy appears an unlikely prospect. Perhaps it is not even desirable. Most population growth in the U.S.A. is immigrant-driven.[69] Such policies would probably generate resentment, based on a sense of (unfair) discrimination. There seems no practicable alternative (as McKibben suggests) to advocating fertility reduction and to working for increased funding for family planning and broader social policies likely to encourage (not compel) fertility-reduction among freely choosing citizens, who will thus be empowered to do what they wish.[70] (Admittedly, how to draw fine distinctions between enticement, persuasion, manipulation, and coercion is unaddressed here.)[71] Bluntly put, there is no point in appealing to nature's imminent "demise" to excuse "stronger measures" if there is no good reason to believe such measures will ameliorate, rather than compound, the planet's problems.

How are we to determine the optimum human population size?[72] It might be claimed that without some target figure, we risk initiating a fertility-decline slippery slope, theoretically if improbably (given govern-

[68]See the discussion in Andrew Dobson, *Green Political Thought*, 2nd ed. (New York: Routledge, 1994), pp. 80-85.

[69]Leon F. Bouvier and Lindsey Grant, *How Many Americans? Population, Immigration and the Environment* (San Francisco: Sierra Club Books, 1994).

[70]McKibben, *Maybe One*, 206-208.

[71]For a discussion in the population context, see John C. Caldwell et al., "Strategies of Fertility Control," in Reich, ed., *The Ethics of Sex and Genetics*, pp. 535-554.

[72]McKibben denies it is possible to do so. He might be correct. *Maybe One*, p. 177. The conceptual problems are analyzed by William Peterson, "History of Population Theories," in Reich, ed., *The Ethics of Sex and Genetics*, p. 498-499. What *exactly* is to be "optimized": number of people, percentage distribution of age groups, etc.?

ment resources to stimulate births) towards human extinction.[73] Some ecophilosophers and scientists have ventured estimates.[74] Of course, any such guideline would have to change as new technologies and attitudes evolve. Nevertheless, without an *approximate* estimate of how many people should dwell on Earth with present or envisageable technology in a minimally harmful manner to nature (and people), a call for fertility reduction lacks an "exit strategy." Surely the public must be convinced that a definitely desirable state will be approached through their self-consciously taken fertility-reduction decisions.

This criticism contains a formidable assumption, for humanity has never existed "harmoniously" with nature, at least not since our very lowest population totals millions of years ago. (And perhaps not even then. Who knows how many local extinctions we caused?) The earliest settlers of the Americas apparently (the thesis is contested) caused massive extinctions.[75] "Descriptions" of indigenous peoples living in harmony with their environments have been shown to be largely products of idealization, ignorance, reverse cultural bias, or the use of them for critical purposes against the critic's own society.[76] If the foundation of natural law is, as it should be, the evidence of biology, anthropology, and other sciences about human nature and conduct, rather than supposedly "self-evident" assertions about human good or the human "condition," some will mistakenly conclude that the natural-law view would be that people should put human welfare ahead of animals'. Accordingly, calls for "sac-

[73]The Swedish government reversed its nation's fertility decline recently. Sarre and Blunder, Eds. *An Overcrowded World?*, p. 127.

[74]An interesting attempt at determining Norway's optimum population is made by (the fascinating) Peter Wessel Zapffe, "Farewell Norway," in Peter Reed and David Rothenberg, eds., *Wisdom in the Open Air: The Norwegian Roots of Deep Ecology* (Minneapolis: The University of Minnesota Press, 1993), pp. 52-59 (tr. Peter Reed). The prospect of reaching a worldwide consensus looks very remote.

[75]A good presentation of the debate will be found in Shepard Kreech III, *The Ecological Indian: Myth and History* (New York: W. W. Norton and Company, 1999). Convinced humans caused most extinctions is Jared Diamond, *Guns, Germs, and Steel* (New York: W. W. Norton and Company, 1998), pp. 42-50.

[76]Especially detailed and telling is Preece, *Animals and Nature*. Also see Kreech III, n. 75 *supra*, and Lawrence H. Keeley, *War Before Civilization: The Myth of the Peaceful Savage* (Oxford: Oxford University Press, 1996).

rificial" conduct will be unlikely to motivate effectively (they rarely do), and attempts to determine an optimum population for nature's sake will be fruitless. The best that could be hoped for is that the self-regarding reasons stimulating decisions for lower fertility (such as mother-child-welfare, higher per-capita incomes, a less crowded world with less crime, pollution, and so on) will also ramify to nature's benefit, as indeed they probably would, should human population decrease dramatically as alternative technologies evolve and simpler lifestyles grow common.

How, in any case, is "harmony" to be interpreted? As with "sustainable development," two possibilities clash. If understood to permit some anthropogenic extinctions, sustainable development will generate controversy over how many, which, and for whose benefits these extinctions should be "allowed." Wide differences over optimum human population size could be expected. Interpret "harmony" more to nature's gain (as restitution for continuing human wrongs mandates), and almost any number of people is too great. If our aim is to preserve other species and organisms, any "greener-than-thou" advocate can demand still steeper fertility reduction to save more of nature.[77] Where (and how) will it stop? Environmentalists must answer this question.

Operationalizing a plausible picture of humanity living in harmony with nature appears impossible.[78] Many people have grown skeptical of utopias too often used as fig leaves to veil the advantages élites gain from imposing hardships on others. Nonetheless, if any substantive progress toward preserving nature is to be made, nations will probably have to reach a consensus on how nature should be managed, and for what goals, in order to facilitate cooperation. Forming this consensus will probably require rejecting the dichotomy implicit in the question: Is it for nature's sake or our own that we undertake to limit our fertility, simplify our lives, and accept less environmentally harmful technology? Broadly speaking, this means that recognition of nature's intrinsic (existence) value should

[77]"Greener than thou" is Stephen J. Gould's expression, on the book cover of the paperback version of Lewis, *Green Delusions*.

[78]Some people try anyway; e.g., Lester Milbrath, *Envisioning a Sustainable Society* (Albany: State University of New York Press, 1989).

itself contribute to the betterment of our lives. Signs that this *is* beginning to happen offer some slight hope for the planet's (and humanity's) long-term well-being.[79]

Deep ecology, from which arose this discussion of the issue of a duty to reduce human population, suggests that the preservation (from humanity) of natural diversity and of the evolutionary process should be an important part of that consensus.[80] Anything less than this would enshrine the very attitude of human "superiority" that has (albeit not alone) led to so many environmental disasters. This criterion leaves room for some (inevitable) human effect on wildlife, although economic critics (like Beckerman) think the criterion would be impossibly demanding.[81] (Some species might inhabit only a small plot of land "required" to provide a clear human benefit, a site for a rural hospital, for example.) How we modify habitats (as well as individual animals and plants) will have to be closely monitored in order that species not be put at much higher risk of extinction than if people did not exist. "Much higher risk" is an elastic expression that hides the enormous impediments to fashioning a way of life that respects the natural tendencies of other living beings equally with the human, as a truly biologically-based natural law obviously should do.[82] To have any hope of achieving this (to the extent possible, i.e., many species beyond saving), human population must decrease. But environmentalism denies that a slowly declining population need simply return,

[79]For one attempt to argue how this can be understood see Peter S. Wenz, *Nature's Keeper* (Philadelphia: Temple University Press, 1996). Claiming that " . . . most Western leaders now recognize that the . . . web of life . . . has its own intrinsic value" is Mary Corliss Pearl, "Ecology and the Environment," in Bulliet, ed., *The Columbia History of the 20th Century*, p. 508. She gives no evidence to support this view, but for what it is worth, I find increasing use of the concept of nature's intrinsic value in public discourse.

[80]Bill Devall and George Sessions, *Deep Ecology* (Salt Lake City: Peregrine Smith Books, 1985), especially pp. 65-76, and, most of all, Arne Naess, *Ecology, Community, and Lifestyle*, tr. and ed. David Rothenberg (Cambridge: Cambridge University Press, 1989).

[81]Wilfred Beckerman, "'Sustainable Development': Is It a Useful Concept?" *Environmental Values* 3 (1994), pp. 191-209; Robert Attfield pens an effective rebuttal in *The Ethics of the Global Environment* (West Lafayette, Indiana: Purdue University Press, 1999), pp. 98-115.

[82]For the difficulties, see Mark A. Michael, ed., *Preserving Wildlife: An International Perspective* (Amherst, NY: Humanity Books, 2000).

as it wanes, to the identical living standard it had as it waxed. Discovering exactly how to live with lighter "footprints" on Earth will take place as the shrinkage occurs, and has already started in the few countries with relatively stable or declining populations.[83]

Natural law has an important role to play in this pragmatic process of determining whether humans can create a balance with nature heretofore unachieved, and indeed its own fate will be determined by it. But playing that role will involve rejecting much of the natural-law "tradition," which has superciliously neglected the equal "right" of all species to exist and to evolve.[84] A biologically grounded natural law would seek a "third way" between human preservation (at nature's expense) and our extinction (for nature's benefit). If natural law's most basic injunction is to live "according to nature" ("what nature teaches all animals," in the words of Justinian's code)[85], then our nature and nature's survival should be compatible, despite all the evidence (not denied here) that they are not. If indeed they are not, then natural law must be summarily rejected, since humanity would have proven itself a freakish misfit, i.e., unfit for any ecological niche. Human "unnaturalness" might, indeed probably will, turn out to be corroborated.[86] But to disconfirm the unnaturalness thesis by acting as if it is false is still a possibility. Should humanity succeed in constructing this "harmony," our "natural piety" would have eventually proven compatible with our species' economic ambitions and social aspi-

[83]Matthis Wackernagel and William E. Rees, *Our Ecological Footprint: Reducing Human Impact on the Earth* (Gabriola Island, B.C.: New Society Publishers, 1996).

[84]Examples, of course, are not proof, but a few will have to do here. "For though man is indeed an animal, he is an extraordinary animal, differing far more from all other animals than they differ in kind from each other." Hugo Grotius, *The Law of War and Peace*, p. 4. Pufendorf, *On the Duty of Man and Citizen*, p. 61: "Man is an animal which is not only intensely interested in its own preservation but also possesses a native and delicate sense of its own value." p. 115: Man should " . . . lead his life in a manner utterly different from that of the animals." In case anyone thinks these attitudes are dead, here is Finnis, *Natural Law and Natural Rights*, pp. 194-195: "Those who propose that animals have rights have a deficient appreciation of human good."

[85]Quoted in and discussed by Stephen R. L. Clark, *Animals and Their Moral Standing* (London: Routledge, 1997), pp. 50-54.

[86]For some attacks on the likelihood of "harmony" between humans and nature (or similar metaphors), see Lewis, *Green Delusions*, pp. 43-81; Matt Ridley, *The Origins of*

rations.[87] Natural law would then have established its own naturalness, i.e., established that the deliverance of practical reasonableness can strengthen rather than weaken our connections to other life forms, evidencing that Earth is where we belong.

Virtue (New York: Viking, 1996), pp. 211-225; John A. Livingston, *Rogue Primate* (Boulder, CO: Roberts Rinehart Publishers, 1994); Michael Tobias, *World War III* (New York: Continuum Publishing Company, 1998). Despite its lurid title, the last book offers convincing reasons to doubt that world population stabilization will be achieved in the 21st century: pp. 233-241. So does historian Roberts, *Twentieth Century*, pp. 39-46, 111-114. (In many parts of the world death rates can still decline enormously; expecting the world to copy Europe's fertility decline is just a hope; many couples still lack access to contraception; many political leaders want higher population growth rates; a huge proportion of the population is just entering its reproductive years; the decline of much of the world into near-anarchy is accelerating, imminent, or likely; etc.)

[87]On such a "piety," see Michael Ignatieff, *The Needs of Strangers* (New York: Viking Press, 1984), p. 139, and Roger Scruton, *An Intelligent Person's Guide to Philosophy* (New York: Penguin, 1998), pp. 117-119.

NATURAL ENVIRONMENT, NATURAL LAW, AND NATURAL SCIENCES—ASPECTS OF A MULTIDISCIPLINARY APPROACH

Guido Leidig

I. INTRODUCTION

If mankind wants to be assured of order in the uncertainty of the world, it is primarily those institutions concerned with law which are called upon to provide the suitable points of orientation. By becoming an institution itself, and succeeding as heir to myth and religion in the central question of what should be considered as an orientation for existence, law was also compelled to take over the authority of its predecessors, which jurisprudence shares. This directly influences the question of how jurisprudence Legal Theory should be able to increase its ability to provide its material—law, also in its practical correctness. The formulation of this question is of particular importance with regard to the ecologic-economic problems to be solved in the highly developed industrial societies. For relationships between the ecological and economic environment are becoming increasingly more complex, and the large amounts of data which describe these relationships are becoming less and less clear to the legislator concerned with environmental law. The growing need for better preparation and for the scientific establishment of environmental laws at all levels, presents the legislator with numerous new functions to which he can scarcely do justice using the traditional methods of jurisprudence. Jurisprudence, therefore, is faced with the demanding task of developing instruments to guide the activities of mankind to a new integration with the natural environment, thus ensuring human survival.[1]

These explanations may be sufficient to show the increasing importance of the function of planning and information in the real process of legislation, which can, according to the theory of communications, be seen as a sequential processing of information.[2] In this context for exam-

[1]G. Leidig, "Environmental Problems and Limitations of Natural Law," *Vera Lex* Volume VII (1988), Nr. 2, p. 15-16, 26. Stober, R, *Handbuch des Wirtschafts-Verwaltungs-und Umweltrechts*, Stuttgart-Berlin-Koln (1989).

[2]G. Leidig, *Okologisch-okonomische Rechtswissenschaft*, Frankfurt/M.-Bern-New York (1984).G. Leidig, *Chaosforschung und Umweltschutz*, Basel (1995).

ple, the significant question for natural law arises from the "subjectivity of nature (natural environment) to law" on the one hand, and of the "rights of future generations" (regarding an ecologically still-intact environment) on the other. These current and scientifically interesting problem areas in the discussion of environmental policy cannot be discussed with finality without a philosophical basis in natural law. These two questions in particular demonstrate the close connection which exists between the problems of environmental protection and natural law.

On the other hand, however, we must ask if a basic position in the philosophy of law, which expects human reason to see meaningful connections, as natural law does, can provide efficient instruments to solve such central problems as environmental protection. Luhmann (1986), for example, takes the view that where nature is concerned, i.e. the preservation of the elements and processes of the natural environment, natural law shows considerable deficits in efficiency. If these deficits are to be eliminated, an ecologic-economic orientation within the framework of jurisprudence is necessary. Otherwise, jurisprudence will not be in a position to satisfactorily solve the current and future tasks set for it.[3] Is this possible without knowledge from Natural Sciences? The answer is no. That's the reason a multidisciplinary approach is necessary—especially with regard to natural law and environmental problems.

II. NATURAL LAW AND MULTIDISCIPLINARY RESEARCH

II.1 *Basic Aspects*

It is evident that a modern and dynamic industrial civilization, undergoing continual development, generates a constant requirement for political steering and problem solving which, however, must have a sufficient theoretical basis if it is to be efficient. Consequently, science finds itself confronted with the problem of supplying adequate answers to the constantly emerging and already-known—but as yet unsolved—key problems of the industrial society, e. g. ecologic and economically connected problem areas. Thus the classical individual sciences—e. g. legal theo-

[3]Leidig, (1984).G. Leidig, "Interdisciplinary Research," in: D. B. S. Fitch/A. Pikalo (Hrsg.), *Soziale und okonomische Aspekte der Bodennutzung*, Frankfurt/M.-Bern-New York-Paris, (1990), 7.

ry—are frequently out of their depth when faced with problems reaching beyond their own disciplines. As theories gleaned from individual sciences are often in no adequate position to record and explain complex problems in ways concurring with reality, the central theme of the question is, therefore, whether the mono-disciplinary research strategy which has been dominant to date should/must be enhanced by a multidisciplinary nature—also, and particularly, with regard to natural law and environmental problems. For it is the key task of science, to provide secure knowledge about the environment and the mechanisms of its functionality. This is being made more difficult at present, as the problem constellations to be solved by science—especially natural sciences—do not adapt themselves to each of the historically grown disciplinary boundaries. They make it necessary for both scientific disciplines and individual researchers to keep an open mind for questions that go beyond a single subject.[4] Is this the next step?

II.2 *New Types of Problems*

From a system-theoretical viewpoint, "environment" is an open, cybernetic, dynamic, complex and less a deterministic system consisting of two major sub-systems of the same structure: the ecological and the anthropogenic. The task of science now lies in describing, explaining, and forecasting the processes within and between these systems. Furthermore, science must provide instruments in order to avoid dysfunctionalities of a system-destructive nature. Here, with regard to the protection of natural resources, for example, numerous disciplines are required—particularly ecology (natural sciences), economics and jurisprudence/legal theory.[5]

[4]G. Leidig, "Ecological Land Development and Multidisciplinary Research," in R. W. Dixon-Gough (Ed.), *Land Reform and Sustainable Development*, Aldershot-Brookfield/USA-Singapore-Sydney, (1999), 43.

[5]G. Leidig, "Chaostheorie und Zukunftsherausforderungen," in: Ch. Bosshardt (Hrsg.), *Problembereiche interdisziplinarer Forschung,* Bern-Berlin-Bruxelles-Frankfurt/M.-New York-Wien, (1999a), 77.G. Leidig, "Rechtsokologische Forschung und Chaostheorie," in: *Zeitschrift fur offentliches Recht* 52, (1997), H. 1, 127.K. Bosselmann, *Okologische Grundrechte*, Baden-Baden, (1998).

In this context, however, the following series of questions is decisive for the prospective orientation of research strategies:

- Are the connections between the effects within one of these systems and between these systems linear and/or non-linear dissipative process structures?

- Are the individual specialist disciplines still able to penetrate such complex problem formations adequately or have the linear standard sciences reached their limits?

- Can non-linear dissipative processes within the sociological system—and their effects on the natural environmental system, to name but one current example—not be dealt with more effectively with a multidisciplinary research strategy and if so what does the necessary metatheoretical foundation look like?[6]

From this point of view it is evident that this kind of system-structures/problems cannot be searched in a mono-disciplinary manner (e. g. by Natural Law) but only interdisciplinary, which is why the following sets out details of some of the central aspects of this approach to research. For in times of fundamental changes—both within our society and in the natural environment—research traditions must be critically queried and if necessary replaced by new approaches. To use same terms developed by Kuhn (1973), many scientific systems are in the "crisis phase" or on the verge of the "revolution phase".

Natural law with regard to finding solutions for environmental problems must use the knowledge of Natural Sciences. One of the most important approaches from this point of view is "Chaos Theory".

II.3 *Necessity of Multidisciplinary Research*

Seen as a whole, there can hardly be a doubt that scientific evolution since the 18th century has brought about ever more tightly defined subdisciplines according to the law of increasing functional inner differenti-

[6]G. Leidig, "Research Strategies in a Time of Change," in: G. M. Schinas/ P. Trappe (Hrsg.), *Gesellschaftssystme im Umbruch-Konsequenzen fur das Eigentum*, Franfurt/M. -Berlin-Bern-New York-Paris-Wien, (1995a), 45.

ation, division of work and specialization.[7] The increasing separation through differentiation of the sub-system science relative to other sociological sub-systems such as the state, religion and art was parallel to the inner differentiation of the sub-system science. Conversely, the ever-present continuing practice-orientation of the sciences pushed towards further specialization. Consequently, both external and internal factors promoted the functional differentiation of science, whereby the external factors were seemingly much more important in the beginning, the internal factors only gaining in relevance during the course of time. Behind the catchword "multidisciplinarity" there are, however, various ideas and approaches which do not all have positive effects on the scientific system. There is, for example, a form of multidisciplinarity which stems from a "disciplinary lack of ideas" which actually supports the continuation of "disciplinary narrow-mindedness." Disciplinary limitations are recognised but not removed, because people only come together for a time, only appear to work beyond their specialist field, but in truth are not prepared to re-think their disciplinary methods and research interests, let alone put them at someone else's disposal.[8] The research strategy becomes bogged down in half-hearted multidisciplinarity.[9]

III. NATURAL LAW AND CHAOS THEORY–THE NEXT STEP?

III.1 *Basic Aspects of Chaos Theory*

III.1.1 Basic Models

In order to master the future challenges of societal systems, a return is needed to holistic research methods and models, which not only incorporate several variables, but also process knowledge from other disciplines integratively and develop them constructively. Chaos theory is

[7]G. Liedig, "Multidisciplinary Research Strategies Using Ecologically Oriented Spatial Planning as an Example," in : T. Tayanna/E. Weiβ (Hrsg.), *Bodenprobleme am Stadtrand*, Frankfurt/M.-Berlin-Bern-New York-Paris-Wien, (1996), 147.

[8]B. Grafrath, R. Huber, B. Uhlemann, *Einheit, Interdisziplinaritat. Orientierungsprobleme der Wissenschaft heute*, Berlin-New York, (1991).

[9]J. Mittelstraβ, "Wohin geht die Wissenschaft?," in: *Konstanzer Blatter fur Hoschschulfragen* 26, (1989), 97.

such an approach: it goes back to a series of basic models stemming from other sciences. It is the product of an innovative process of synthesis. The central "basic components" can—with regard to their most important knowledge—be described as follows:[10]

a) System Theory

Von Bertalanffy (1968) is generally considered to be the first to formulate a comprehensive theoretical system of thought, which describes the organizational principles of living systems. This approach realizes that not only individual elements but also interdependencies between these are essential for a comprehensive scientific understanding of problem networks; a component which chaos theory goes back to and combines with other knowledge.

A similar approach to that of von Bertalanffy was developed about 30 years earlier by the Russian scientist Alexander Bogdano,[11] which he called tectology, the "science of structures." His main aim was the determination and generalization of organizational principles of all living and non-living structures. Both models contain central basic knowledge, which were integrated into chaos theory.

b) Cybernetics

This line of thought, developed by Wiener (1948), a field of science going beyond the classical boundaries, examines a phenomenon existing in natural and anthropogenic systems, namely the steering, i.e. the "keeping under control" of conditions. Central to the development of chaos theory was a line of thought pertaining to circular systems with a feedback-effect as defined in cybernetics. This general principle of regulated cycles can, despite its high degree of abstraction, be used for the explanation of processes in the natural or artificial environment (e.g. cycle of nature, cycle of economics).

c) Self-Organization Theory

The principle of self-organization is another main component of chaos theory. It means that in a system without external influences, structures

[10]Leidig, (1995), Leidig, (1997), 127, Leidig, (1999), 43, Leidig, (1999a), 77. J. Briggs and F. Peat, *Turbulent Mirror*, New York, Harper & Row, (1989). P. Davies, *Prinzip Chaos*, 3. Aufl., Stuttgart, (1988). F. Cramer, *Chaos und Ordnung*, 3. Aufl., Stuttgart, (1989).

[11]G. Gorelik, "Principal Ideas of Bogdanov's Tectology: the Universal Science of Organization," in *General Systems*, (1994), Bd. XX, 3.

form the characteristic in which both its organization and order increase. Self-organization in stages of societal development takes place in particular in a period of change. Koselleck (1972) understands this to mean historical periods in which a modification of central norms and values of a society take place so that the system is in a phase of radical change marked by a high potential for chaos in which concepts such as planning and controllability fail to a large degree. At this "threshold," according to Mittelstaedt (1997), self-organizing mechanisms occur which form new structures from the period of radical change or from chaos.

d) Ecological Research

Building on Darwinian ideas Haeckel (1866) realized that the structure of reciprocal relationships of species can become knowledge of a new scientific discipline and coined the name "ecology" for it. This approach researches the environmental factors influencing organisms as well as the living requirements of certain species and the demands these make on the environment. In view of the problems to be discussed here, the "deep ecology"[12] approach is of interest. It sees neither mankind nor anything else as being separated from the natural environment. It does not see in the world a collection of objects isolated from each other but a network of phenomena which are basically connected to each other and are mutually dependent on each other: a point of view which was adopted by chaos theory.

e) Theory of "Dissipative Structures"

The theory shows that the behavior of a dissipative structure far from the equilibrium no longer follows any universal law. Near the equilibrium repeating phenomena and universal laws can be found. However, as soon as we move away from the equilibrium, we move from the universal to the singular, to abundance and variety.[13] The existence of forks (bifurcations) means that uncertainty is another characteristic of this approach. At each bifurcation, a central mechanism in chaos theory, there is a non-reducible element of chance. Which way the system will take depends on its own history and cannot be predicted.

[12]J. Heinrichs, *Okologik. Tiefenololigie als strukturelle Naturphilosophie*, Frankfurt/M.-Berlin-Bern-New York-Paris-Wien, (1997). F. Capra, *Lebensnetze*, Bern-Munchen-Wien, (1996).

[13]Capra, (1996).

f) Autopoiesis Approach

Maturana/Varela (1980) developed the theory of autopoiesis, the organisational pattern of living systems. The notion of autopoiesis, the property of living systems, is to constantly renew itself and to regulate this process in such a way that the integrity of the structure is preserved. Autopoiesis is described as a network pattern in which each component has the function of participating in the transformation or production of other components.

III.1.2 Components/Mechanisms

Unlike many classical disciplines chaos theory does not reduce objects of research to ideal cases which do not exist in reality. It accepts disruptive factors as normal, as a natural process and sees the occurrence—for example, the interwovenness of the anthropogenic and the natural environment—in its overall complexity. Chaotic behavior can be found in almost all areas. Identifying chaos is in many cases not a part of scientific research, or is only in its beginnings. In order to create a basis for further investigations, the central components and mechanisms must briefly be systematised.[14]

a) Components

aa) Chaos

The term 'chaos' originates from the Greek and literally translated means "structureless primordial mass." All creation myths begin with chaos, the Big Bang, the primordial sea from which the world and life originated. However, chaos should not be mistaken for anarchy, lawlessness, disorder or lack of rules. Chaos research—in the sense of mathematical theory—is seen as the study of disorder occurring in nonlinear systems and the search for new terms of classification. Chaos theory, then, deals with the conditions under which chaos occurs, the exact characteristics and the effects of chaotic movements as well as the values of its limits. These examinations take place both in concrete systems (e.g. the ecosystem) and using mathematical models.

[14]Leidig, (1999a), 77.

bb) Characteristics

The dominant characteristics of chaotic processes can be shown as follows:

• *Inseparable association with non-linearity*

Here chaos can even exist/occur in very simple non-linear dynamic systems.

• *Sensitive dependency on initial conditions*

This means that adjacent starting points lead to a completely different sequence of condition variables after a finite time whereby movement in the non-linear dissipative systems observed here remains globally limited, unlike in the case of unstable dynamic systems.

• *Sensitive dependency on control parameters*

This leads to an infringement of the causality principle because similar causes no longer have similar effects.

• *Irregularity of movement*

Chaotic movements do not follow a simple pattern but proceed irregularly over a broad field of frequency.

• *Incalculable long-term behavior*

This results from the general knowledge of the initial quantities and the model equations since very small measuring errors in the initial conditions as well as tiny disruptions along chaotic trajectories will increase. In this way new errors are added to the old with the slightest external influence so that the overall error quotient is multiplied and slight deviations rapidly take on large dimensions.

• *Order in chaos*

Chaotic systems and their movements can be quantitatively characterized with the help of new terms of classification, which are closely associated with self-similarity, scale-invariance and universality. On the one hand it can thereby be demonstrated that different non-linear systems behave in a similar fashion when crossing over from ordered structures to chaos. On the other hand, ordered structures can even be demonstrated in chaos.[15]

[15]Leidig, (1999a), 77.

b) Mechanisms

aa) Non-linearity

However, non-linear systems—and these should be dominant in reality—have until now for the most part been neglected within the framework of scientific research efforts, even with regard to the shaping of instruments for environmental protection. In a non-linear system, a complex ecosystem, the whole is far more than the sum of its parts. Linear models fail because they are unable to record what is significant—the totality of interdependencies between the elements and processes of sensitive dynamic structures.[16]

bb) Bifurcations

Bifurcations are the milestones in system evolution: history crystallizes in them. In the development of a system a bifurcation is that decisive moment at which slight changes bring about a branching from the previous 'path' and the system moves in a new direction. Over the course of time whole cascades of bifurcation points either cause a system to split up into chaos or—through a sequence of feedback loops which combine the latest changes with the surroundings—to stabilize in new behavior. In the area of those points in which the "memory" of past bifurcations has crystallized, systems usually remain very sensitive.[17]

cc) Feedback

Feedback describes the connection between cause, effect, and response in a system. We speak of positive feedback when the effect and the response strengthen each other. Negative feedback is when the effect and the response weaken each other. This is the basic principle of all circuits. Systems only remain in a stable condition through negative feedback. This mechanism must be taken into consideration in conceiving instruments for environmental protection; until now, however, this has been ignored in many cases.

III.1.3 Conclusions

Chaos research is also giving innovative impetus to Legal Theory which alternatives must thereby be strategically considered and held in readiness. In the end, only one of the alternative actions will be carried

[16]Leidg, (1999a), 77.

[17]Leidig, (1995). Leidig, (1999a), 77.

out. Due to the uncertainty of non-linear systems assumed in chaotic processes, it is not possible to make clear forecasts.[18] Non-linear models no longer model all the individual causal chains but knots in which feedback loops interconnect. The goal is not a forecast but a means of disrupting the model by varying the parameters, thereby learning something about the critical points of the system and about its capability for resistance.

Analogies of the working mechanisms, from the perspective of Legal Theory and environmental law, show that relationships do exist. This means that the chaos-theoretical approach in jurisprudence certainly comes into its own. It was, of course, possible to give plausible reasons for development processes before now. In this way for example, the necessity for development measures was derived from the ageing process of extremely interwoven systems without the ability of self-regeneration. Here, however, chaos theory opens up new perspectives for Legal Theory. For example, crises emerge in points of bifurcation, but in their proximity the systems mostly remain very sensitive. Our legal systems are in a dynamic relation of change and stability.

The investigation of chaos and its working mechanisms strengthens the initial theory of a holistic approach, e.g. within ecologically oriented jurisprudence or natural law. In this context, chaos theory provides new patterns of thought and research whose potential should not remain unused. Natural law needs the knowledge of this approach, to find solutions for ecologically oriented problems in a changing world. Without this information, the efficiency of solutions is not very high.

III.2 *Fields of Application*

From the above discourse on chaos theory, the following conclusions present themselves for mastering future demands with regard to the early recognition and steering of ecologic-economically interwoven fields of crisis:[19]

> •Particularly in complex dynamic systems, even slight non-linearity can trigger chaotic behavior. Testing should in future be performed on the basis of dynamic models (e.g. using simulations) before making deci-

[18] Leidig, (1997), 127.
[19] Leidig, (1999a), 77. Leidig, (1997), 127.

sions influencing natural or societal systems, to see whether the parameters which have the most influence on the behavior of the system are close to areas of chaotic values.

•Moreover, critical system parameters in the case of decisions close to areas of chaotic values must be constantly checked in order to prevent them, through appropriate measures, from sliding into the regime of the chaotic.

•An absolute prerequisite for the introduction of such ecological strategies for avoiding crises is that the non-linearity generating the chaotic behavior and the constellation of parameters decisive for the behavior of the system are recognized at an early stage and chaotic developments can be identified as such.

•Further progress in this extremely interesting field for the avoidance of crises and the mastering of the future can be expected when the presence of non-linearity can be successfully detected, perhaps by the systematic evaluation of available data and the further development in the case of chaotic behavior can be forecast better.

That means that natural law needs information from other sciences to produce efficient solutions. One important approach is Chaos Theory.[20]

SUMMARY

It can be seen to an increasing degree that a modern, dynamic and continually developing industrial society has a constant requirement for scientific-political solutions to problems. Consequently, the scientific system sees itself confronted with the problems of developing adequate concepts for solving the newly emerging and already known—but as yet mainly unsolved—central problems of industrial sociological systems; for example, the maintaining of natural resource potentials. However, this goal can only be realized with a multidisciplinary research strategy, which is not limited to a passive registration and passive synthesizing of single pieces of knowledge from other sciences. But it is seen as an attempt to integrate different disciplinary approaches to solving problem areas, while aspiring to achieve a deeper understanding and penetration of the fields of research to be analyzed. It is particularly for this reason

[20]Leidig, (1999), 43.

that such a strategy, aspiring to integrate knowledge from specific disciplines, is becoming increasingly significant. Compared to the disciplinary research strategy, the multidisciplinary approach to research has the decisive advantage that it is better adapted to the essence and the complexity of reality. However, this does not mean that the multidisciplinary approach to research will become an alternative to monodisciplinary (pertaining to one field) research. It is rather a sensible, because necessary, extension thereof. There exists a close factual relationship between the two research methods: monodisciplinary research is a prerequisite for multi/interdisciplinary research, which, for its part, can give new impetus to the disciplinary form. For it is not the aim of the multi/interdisciplinary research strategy to do away with specialization in the development of the sciences, but to overcome and avoid closed off and isolated "research in an ivory tower." The task of the multidisciplinary research strategy—like the monodisciplinary strategy—is to develop new theoretical concepts, which permit us to come closer to solving the problems of our sociological system.

REFERENCES

L. V. Bertalanffy
Generals Systems Theory, New York 1968.

E. Haeckel
Generelle Morphologie der Organismen, Bd. 2, Berlin 1866.

J. Heinrichs
Ökologik. Tiefenökologie als strukturelle Naturphilosophie, Frankfurt/M. – Berlin – Bern – New York – Paris – Wien 1997.

R. Koselleck
Über die Theoriebedürftigkeit der Geschichtswissenschaft, in:
P. Böhning (Hrsg.), Geschichte und Sozialwissenschaften, Göttingen 1972, p. 18 pp.

T. S. Kuhn
Die Struktur wissenschaftlicher Revolutionen, Frankfurt/M. 1973.

H. Maturana/F. Varela
Autopoiesis and Cognition, Dordrecht 1980.

W. Mittelstaedt
Der Chaos-Schock und die Zukunft der Menschheit, Frankfurt/M. – Berlin – Bern – New York – Wien 1997.

N. Wiener
Cybernetics. Or control and communication in the animal and the machine, New York 1948.

PRACTICAL REASON, PERSON AND COMMON GOOD

Alejandra Carrasco

Law is an ordinance of reason for the Common Good, promulgated by him who has the care of the community.
(*Sum. theol. i-ii. 90.4*, trans. A.C. Pegis)

The notion of Common Good as the final cause of law was, for the classics, the concept that illuminated their interpretation of society and of individual human beings. This notion, however, is not completely intelligible to the Modern mind and its role in political theory is thus undervalued, with detrimental consequences in our culture. In these pages I will suggest that the reason for this phenomenon is that the notion of "Common Good" is a matter of practical reason. During Modernity, due to different historical circumstances, technical reason gradually took the place of practical reason in Ethics and Politics, and the legitimacy of practical reason started to be questioned. Obviously, this trespassing of operational spheres could not be innocuous; rather, the "technification" of morality and politics has completely changed our concepts of law, person and community.

Although all generalizations are necessarily simplifications, in this essay I will understand by "Modern mind" the powerful stream of thought born from the seventeenth century scientific and philosophical revolution and later materialized in different kinds of empiricisms, mechanicisms, idealisms and voluntarisms. Despite the significant differences among these systems, they all share an empiric-mathematical discourse, a manifest admiration of the progress of basic sciences, and they discredit the classical metaphysical concept of nature. The intellectual victory of these modern systems was supported, in the popular culture, by the benefits of scientific technology which promoted the "commodiousness of humanity."[1] Hence the hegemony of this mentality and the current lack of an adequate foundation for notions such as Common Good, teleology, natural law, and many others which help to understand the meaning of personhood and to politically promote a real "human" society.

[1]Cf. Kenneth Schmitz, "Postmodernism and Catholic Tradition," *American Catholic Philosophical Quarterly*, vol. LXXIII, n2, Spring 1999, p.241

Notwithstanding, after centuries of Modernity and the possibility of a dispassionate evaluation of its achievements, it may be time to retrieve those forgotten concepts and try to re-understand them in the light of our present reality. Undoubtedly Aristotle and Thomas Aquinas are the sources *par excellence* in this topic, although recourse to contemporary scholars is always helpful to apply their thought to our world. My aim in this essay, therefore, will be to try to make intelligible and thus to vindicate the notion of Common Good, in order to recognize it as a credible *telos* for law and society. Nonetheless, this aim requires to recall first the main differences between the forgotten practical and the currently hegemonic technical reason. This will also bring to the foreground the concept of person in all its objective dignity. It is necessary, then, to show in what sense the Common Good is essentially a matter of practical reason, and why it can be defined and adequately characterized only within the sphere of this mode of thinking, with all the peculiarities and possibilities this horizon offers. The Common Good, indeed, is the social expression of what is called "happiness" or *eudaimonia* in Aristotle's Ethics. In other words, the Common Good is the end of man-in-society, the primary cause and the source of all meaning for people's coordinated action. Rediscovering some of its potentialities, then, may bring some fresh air to the exhausted modern political theory.

I. PRACTICAL REASON AND MODERN MIND

According to Aristotle, there are three different modes in which human reason may operate, and the object of reason determines which is appropriate in each case. When the aim is truth for its own sake, the activity is called *theoria* or science. When it is action, as in Ethics and Politics (people leading their lives), practical reason heads *praxis*. And when the aim is a product, an external object, the activity is *poiesis* and reason operates technically.[2] Concretely, technical reason identifies a particular and partial good, and chooses the most efficient means to achieve it.

Each of these spheres has different laws of operation, and despite that there is only one reason (one faculty), the mode of operation specifies the

[2]Aristotle, *Ethica Nicomachea*, translated by W.D. Ross, Oxford University Press, 1925, Book VI,4 (1140a).

goal, the characteristics and elements that must be considered in the process, along with the legitimate way of verification. For instance, Aristotle, distinguishing spheres, says: "Practical wisdom cannot be scientific knowledge nor art; not science because that which can be done is capable of being otherwise, not art because action and making are different kinds of things."[3] Other relevant differences between these three modes of reason are: the kind of action they mainly deal with (*poiesis* deals with transitive actions while *praxis* and *theoria* with immanent actions, i.e. actuality in the thing made or actuality in the agent, respectively);[4] their degree of communicability (techniques and sciences insofar as they are directly or indirectly dominated by technical purposes are highly communicable, while practical judgement is *per se* incommunicable); and their relation to the principles: in human acts ends are what principles are in speculative matters.[5] Therefore, as it can be easily seen, there are real and crucial differences between these three modes of reason, which make them irreducible to each other.

I.1. *Difficulties of practical reason in modern times*

Due to the predominant paradigm of knowledge in Modernity, and despite its essential differences with the other modes of reason, practical reason has gradually become obscure to our mind. One of its features most negatively relevant to modern comprehension is personal reference. The other two modes of reason, theoretical and technical, refer primarily to the object and only indirectly to the subject of action or agent. *Praxis* is different. The subject or agent under this mode of reason is at the same time—although not always immediately—the object of the action.[6] Therefore, he can never be detached or disengaged from it. And this unavoidable presence of the subject *qua* subject is an especially prob-

[3]Aristotle, *Ethica Nicomachea*, Book VI, 5 (1140b40-43).

[4]Cf. Aristotle, *Metaphysics*, translated by W.D. Ross, Book IX, 8 (1050a30).

[5]Cf. Aristotle, *Ethica Nicomachea*, Book VII, 8 (1151a16).

[6]Reflexivity is not always "immediate reflexivity." The agent may act over himself, over another subject or over an object; nonetheless, the particularity of *praxis* is that the action will always be directed back upon the doer. In this sense, mediately or immediately, he is the object of his own action.

lematic feature for, for example, the ideals of neutrality or impersonality of the modern paradigm of knowledge based on the model of Natural Sciences.

Another essential characteristic of practical reason that does not fit in the modern paradigm of knowledge is its *constitutive relation to the good*, in the sense that all the *raison d'être* of *praxis* is to achieve the good of man, of the concrete person (or community) who is reasoning. Consequently, practical reason is moral reason, a reason that does not seek a particular or instrumental good like technical reason, but rather the good as such, the good-without-qualifications of the person. Practical reason does not seek to improve an aspect, but the person as a person.

Furthermore, the very way of proceeding and mode of verification of practical reason are not transparent to the Post-scientific-revolution mind, which seeks certitude and logical necessity. Practical reasoning, unlike theoretical and technical, is "a reasoning in transitions. It aims to establish, not that some position is correct absolutely, but rather that some position is superior to some other."[7] It involves a continuous transition towards an increasingly perspicuous interpretative stance, and its conclusions are in some sense unique, unprecedented and unrenewable, for they involve reference to all contingencies of particular situations. Practical discourse, unlike theoretical and technical, essentially embraces singularity and contingency.[8] Consequently, and also because human beings are "self interpreting animals"[9] who are permanently reevaluating and rearticulating their understanding of themselves and of the situation, moral or practical sciences cannot intend the same kind of necessity, objectivity and universality as theoretical sciences.

I will later say more about practical knowledge. For now, let us just say that its way of proceeding is more prudential than logical, and therefore its mode of verification is also different and especially problematic to our Modern mind. While for *theoria* verification comes from logic and

[7]Charles Taylor, *Sources of the Self*, Harvard University Press, Massachusetts, 1989, p.72.

[8]Cf. Ives Simon, *The Tradition of Natural Law*, ed. Vukan Kuic, Fordham University Press, New York, 1992.

[9]See C. Taylor, *Philosophy and the Human Sciences*, Cambridge UP1985, Chapter 1: "Interpretation and the Sciences of Man," pp.15-57.

for *poiesis* it comes from efficacy, *praxis* is verified by a more subtle and non-generalist norm, something like "acting according to what is reasonable to achieve the good of the person".

Therefore, practical reason is not able to give absolute or uniform answers whatever the circumstances. On the contrary, the canon is "to act prudently"; yet as G. E. M. Anscombe says in her famous essay "Modern Moral Philosophy," that canon "of course is not a canon."[10] In other words, according to practical reason "to each is to be attributed that which is proper to each and pertains to each"[11] and no a priori answer can be set, as modern paradigms of knowledge demand. Indeed, modern empiricism and rationalism do intend absolute certainty, even in matters unable to give it at all or in terms of the modern ideals of verification (logic and brute data). As Charles Taylor sensibly observes about the modern model of practical reason, it is based "on an illegitimate extrapolation from reasoning in natural sciences."[12] The kind of universality that may be asked to the sphere of *praxis* is, of course, different from the one in *theoria*.[13] There are questions which call for treatment in terms of prudence and cannot be treated in terms of law, asking of them the universality proper to the necessity of essences. The ideal of a social science or a system of laws that would give in each particular case a rational universal solution is deceptive. Only prudence can fill the gap between the universal and the particular. Law—and finally natural law—is the premise of practical judgement and not its conclusion.

I.2 *Telos*

Another major difficulty of practical reason when faced with the Modern mind is the notion of *telos*. I treat this point separately not only because of its importance, but also for the many consequences this notion will have on the comprehension of the Common Good. Aristotelian *telos*

[10]G. E. M. Anscombe, "Modern moral philosophy," in Hudson, W.D. (ed.), *The Is-Ought Question*, Macmillan St Martin's Press, 1969, p.191.

[11]Aquinas, *St. Thomas Aquinas on Aristotle's Love and Friendship, E.N. Books VIII and IX*, translated by Pierre Conway, O.P., The Providence College Press, 1951, p.129.

[12]C. Taylor, *Sources of the Self*, p.7.

[13]Among other things, practical reason must also include particulars. Cf. *Ethica Nicomachea*, VI,7 (1141b15).

differs from modern concepts of *telos* in many ways, and it is important to understand the first notion because it is the only one able to give meaning—ontological, normative and operational meaning—to the Common Good. For Aristotle, *telos* is the perfection/perfect completion of each essence, and as such it is the proper good of that nature. During Modernity the concept of *end*, even called *telos* many times, has different characteristics. For Consequentialism it is a product, a technical (external) good, related with desires rather than perfection of nature. Hegel disregards the plurality of essences, focusing on the *telos* of the Geist. And for Kant the *ends* are regulative but not constitutive of nature; they are ideals of reason rather than objective achievable reality. There are countless other systems, but none of them capture the core of the classic *telos*. When A. MacIntyre says that Liberalism has replaced the Aristotelian "good" by "goods", and thus has impeded the Aristotelian unambiguous practical reasoning,[14] he is precisely pointing out two of the big difficulties of legitimating the activity of practical reason in our times. First, the darkness of the Aristotelian good understood as a *telos*, and second, its replacement by a series of concrete, material and sometimes incompatible (non *telos*) goods.

Without a correct comprehension of the *telos*, then, in its descriptive and normative sense, it is not possible to understand practical reason. And this is because all praxis' meaning, legitimacy and strength come from that primary notion. The *telos*—the absolute good of the person—simultaneously shows and indicates the model or ideal towards which a specific being tends, and gives the criterion for moral evaluation of his/her actions. In Aristotle's Ethics, this primary notion, the *telos* that expresses the plenitude and perfect self-realization of men, is called "happiness." In Politics, i.e. when we consider men living together and not individually, this same notion is the Common Good. Despite its appearance, this "double human *telos*" is materially one and only one, although it is formally two. To understand this distinction requires three brief steps. First, to specify the meaning of "happiness" as ultimate end and indicate its fundamental role in the articulation of Ethics. Second, to acknowledge the

[14]See A. McIntyre, "The privatization of the good", in C. F. Delaney, (ed.), *The Liberalism-Communitarianism Debate*, Rowman and Littlefield Publishers, 1994, p.10.

fact that Politics is also a matter of practical reasoning. And finally, to conclude that "Common Good" is the name of man's single *telos* when considered within the *polis*. Moreover, and because it is the same, the Common Good should have the same character and properties as "happiness" in Ethics.

I.2.1 Meaning of Aristotle's *telos*[15]

The first point, then, is to clarify the meaning of "happiness" as the end of man. Aristotle, in the first book of *Ethica Nicomachea*, argues that the end of man shall be something desired for its own sake and not for the sake of something else. This "thing" is, obviously, "happiness." Thus, the problem now is to define "happiness." As the superior good, it must imply the complete development of man's potentialities, especially of his highest faculty: reason. Therefore, for Aristotle "happiness" is life according to reason, i.e. good life or virtuous life. In his own words: "Human good turns out to be the activity of the soul in accordance with virtue, and if there are more than one virtue, in accordance to the best and most complete. But we must add 'in a complete life.'"[16] This concept is the one that illuminates and gives sense to practical reasoning, for every judgement should be made in reference to this last end.

Clearly, in this treatise the philosopher is neither talking of happiness as emotional satisfaction, a specific value that should be maximized, nor a set of concrete values that should be achieved in some proportion. These three possibilities would be an object for technical reason, a desired product obtained through the most efficient process. Rather, the classic *telos* is a tendency and directive ideal, a possible though extreme-

[15]There is a well-known discussion about the correct interpretation of "the human good" in Aristotle. I will take here the position of Richard Kraut, who rejects the sometimes called "inclusivist view." This interpretation says that happiness is the most choiceworthy good because of its all-inclusive structure: all compossible intrinsic goods are included within it, so that there is no way to make it more desirable by adding something else to it. Kraut, on the contrary, believes that happiness is more than a list of intrinsic goods, for we must determine which of them is most worthwhile and how much each should be pursued. Happiness is the end for the sake of which all other goods are desired, and it consists solely in virtuous activity, not in a composite of all intrinsic goods. See especially Richard Kraut, *Aristotle on the Human Good*, Princeton University Press, New Jersey, 1989.

[16]Aristotle, *Ethica Nicomachea*, Book I, 8 (1097b17-19).

ly difficult task—for it compromises the whole person—which includes the acquisition and exercise of different virtues in the adequate proportion to the particular circumstances of everyone, and during a complete life. It is like a model that can be incarnate in indefinite though not infinite ways, because it is essentially something very definite: it is a good. Further, it is the "complete good," emerging from the achievement of many other goods[17] and their order, i.e. the articulation of these goods in some proportion. Therefore, and because it is a good, the *telos* is, on the one hand, desirable, and on the other, perfective of human nature. "Happiness" is not only a descriptive concept, but it is also a normative concept, a criterion for moral evaluation. Moreover, *telos* is not external to each subject. It is already somehow potentially contained in our very being.

I.2.2. Politics as practical science

The second necessary step to identify in some sense "happiness" and Common Good, is to show the relation between Politics and Ethics. In the horizon of Classic Philosophy, Politics is not the science that studies the competition for state-power but the continuation of Ethics in another sphere, namely, the study of human action within the *polis*, and thus ordered to achieve not only the good of the person but the good of the whole (the community of persons). Aristotle is very clear: "Since happiness is an activity of the soul in accordance with perfect virtue, we must consider the nature of virtue, for perhaps we shall see thus the nature of happiness. The true student of politics, too, is thought to have studied virtue above all things; for he wishes to make his fellow citizens good and obedient to law."[18] Therefore, just as in Ethics the *telos* is the good life and the means to reach it is the operation of our practical mode of reasoning, in Politics the *telos* will be the good life of society[19] and the means will also be the good exercise of practical reason. In this field, where several people and their relations are considered, instead of talking of "personal happiness," we talk of "common happiness," common *eudaimonia* or, what is the same, Common Good. Thus, by Common Good we understand exactly the same perfective happiness we described

[17]Cf. Aristotle, *Ethica Nicomachea*, Book I, 2 (1184a14-35).

[18]Aristotle, *Ethica Nicomachea*, Book I, 13 (1102a5-10).

[19]Cf. Aristotle, *Politics*, Book I, 1 (1252a3-6).

for Ethics: just as the life of one individual is intrinsically oriented towards the complete development of his potentialities as its practical end and all his/her actions make full sense in light of this *telos*; life of society is oriented to the Common Good.[20] Furthermore, the bond among people in community is "concord," i.e. the agreement of the members in relation to practical ends: "things that are in our interest and have influence in our lives."[21]

I.2.3. Material identification and consequences

Consequently, it seems fairly evident that happiness and Common Good are materially the same, despite their formal differences. Aristotle says "Political wisdom and practical wisdom are the same state of mind, but their essence is not the same."[22] Following the same tradition, Jacques Maritain affirms that the Common Good is "communion in good living"[23] and its characteristic feature is the reciprocal help of fellowmen in doing the work of reason and virtue, which correspond to the specific feature of the human being.[24] In this sense, Maritain clearly identifies the Common Good with that "happiness" that crowns the virtuous life. While one is "the good of the most complete society," the other is "the good of the individual."[25] Therefore, and in spite of their formal differences—reference to community or to a single person—these notions are materially the same.

Furthermore, from this material identification, we can bring out some consequences that will clarify the meaning and function of the Common Good. First of all, given the correspondence between the common and the personal good, it is quite evident that they can never oppose each other. The Common Good cannot, without conceptual contradiction, threaten

[20]Other passages where Aristotle asserts that the life of virtue is not only the best life for the individual but the best life of the city are *Politics*, Book VII, 1 (1323a14) and (1323b38).

[21]Aristotle, *Ethica Nicomachea*, Book IX, 6 (1167b4).

[22]Aristotle, *Ethica Nicomachea*, Book VI, 8 (1141b23). Also see I, 3 (1094b7) and *Politics*, VII, 2 (1324a5-14).

[23]Jacques Maritain, *The Person and the Common Good*, translated by John J. Fitzgerald, Charles Scribner Press, 1947, p.40.

[24]J. Maritain, p.38.

[25]Cf. I. Simon, p.87.

the accomplishment of personal happiness, of the good of the person, even though it might ask considerable sacrifices.[26] Indeed, if the Common Good is not universal, namely absolutely good for everyone, it is not a legitimate Common Good. The "good" is not a genus divided in two species, personal and common, which may be opposed. Rather, the "good" is a transcendental, with the universality proper to transcendentals, which unify the being in their very notion. Therefore, if a specific community is unable to take into account the plenitude of man, offering him the means to accomplish his proper end, clearly the Common Good it proclaims is not a perfect, or even a real, Common Good.[27] The genuine Common Good, then, far from the modern misinterpretations of it (external good, useful good, potentially undistributed goods), has for its most essential and significant feature, in fact, to reside *in* men.

A second consequence of this material identification is that, in spite of being the same "good," if the Common Good is perfect Common Good, it is superior to personal good. The reason is easy to understand. Personal and Common Good are the same, as individual happiness and shared happiness are the same. But shared happiness is better, not only because of the number (a greater number of happy individuals is better than less, and a larger amount of goods is better than less) but because of another perfection. Aristotle already said it: "For even if the end is the same for a single man and for a state, that of the state seems at all events something greater and more complete whether to attain or to preserve."[28] The new perfection of the Common Good, then, is that it gives origin to community, in other words, to an order of individuals that not only possess their particular goods but also the good of the whole.[29] Consequently, the sum of particular goods is less valuable than the Common Good, because the last one is the good *in* community, the good realized in a new dimension, a dimension that is impossible to achieve for individuals alone

[26]Cf. Karol Wojtyla, "Thomistic Personalism" in *Person and Community*, translated by Theresa Sandok, O.S.M., Ed. Peter Lang, 1993, p.174.

[27]Carlos Cardona, *La Metafísica del Bien Común*, Ed. Rialp, 1966, p.79.

[28]Aristotle, *Ethica Nicomachea*, Book I, 3 (1094b7-9). Also in *Ethica Nicomachea* I, 2 (1094b7) he describes the good of the city as "greater and more divine". The reasons Ives Simon gives for this primacy are three: completeness, duration and distribution.

[29]C. Cardona, pp.44-47.

and that perfects and further develops them as *persons*. The Common Good adds to the personal good something it cannot have by itself.

A third consequence of this identification is that, just as "happiness" cannot be defined as a fixed set of values, the perfection of society, the Common Good, also cannot be exhausted in a list of goods. It contains numerous and incommensurable goods, which may be realized in also indefinite ways, but it should not be identified with them.

Therefore, the Common Good is not a single specific collective goal (like the utilitarian maximization of happiness-pleasure), or the (subjective) "common interest" of society, or welfare, or even Locke's ideal of defending property in a broad sense. All that is too little for the Common Good and it misses its central dimension. The Common Good is the absolute good, the good "for its own sake," and thus the end capable of giving sense to social life, of making life a totality of meaning. It is a regulative ideal in light of which all particular decisions are made, and the source of meaning for those decisions and actions. But the Common Good is neither a core of shared values that may be theoretically exposed, as some communitarians proclaim, nor the liberal "reflective equilibrium" that harmonizes everybody's interests, nor even the liberal and libertarian minimal conditions necessary for the full development or expansion of individuals. The Common Good is more; it is the actual realization of the full development of individuals. The bare conditions for it are instrumental goods, efficient goods; instead, the Common Good is an absolute good because it is a moral (and not a technical) notion.

Moreover, and even if it is empirically difficult (though not logically impossible) to steadily realize this absolute good, it is always the ideal towards which society should tend, and, more important, the reference for discriminating good and bad actions. This ideal must play the role of a heuristic guide in social decisions,[30] though not merely as unachievable Kantian transcendental ideas, for the *telos* is not only regulative but constitutive of nature.

Thus, when modern liberal philosophers contrast political conceptions of justice between the ones that believe in the existence of "many

[30]Jude Dougherty, "Tener en Mente el Bien Común", *Ethos*, vol.12-13, 1984-1985, p.145.

incommensurable goods" and the ones that postulate "one *summum bonum*,"[31] if they understood the latter as the Common Good, there is no reason to find contradiction. There will be contradiction only if that *summum bonum* is defined on the same level as the other many goods, but not if it is defined as the partial realization of those incommensurable values in an adequate proportion in order to allow the emergence of social *eudaimonia*, of the living well of society or, what is the same, life according to the reason/virtue of its citizens. In other words, if this same argument was understood with practical reason instead of technical reason, there should be no problem. The "moral pluralism" Liberalism promotes, erecting itself as the only system capable to understand and realize a social unity given incommensurable goods[32], is not an inconvenience, *per se*, for the doctrine of the Common Good.

II. FORMALITIES OF THE COMMON GOOD AS A CONCEPT OF PRACTICAL REASON

The understanding of the Common Good as a concept of practical reason has unavoidable consequences, which shall be pointed out in order to re-understand and try to vindicate its legitimacy as a key concept for the political world, not only political theory but mainly political practice. The peculiar parameters and characteristics of practical reason provide a special form to the concept of Common Good; they print on it some intrinsic formalities that otherwise could be accidental. Specifically, the characteristics of this mode of thinking that I want to highlight when it is used to direct political life are: Morality, Plausibility and Teleology. Moreover, since the Common Good is the *telos* of political life, these peculiarities are imprinted in its very notion, and their correct understanding is essential to appreciate the meaning of the Common Good in all its richness and operativeness. Among these three features, Morality is the basis, and it may be even said that it is the nature of the Common Good. Plausibility indicates the way of verification in this sphere of knowledge. And Teleology, although not a necessary feature of moral jus-

[31]Cf. John Rawls, "Justice as Fairness: Political Not Metaphysical", *Philosophy and Public Affairs*, vol.14, 1985, p.248ff.

[32]Cf. J. Rawls.

tification as such for a moral theory may also be deontological, is a necessary element in a theory of the Common Good insofar as every good is an end.

II.1 *Morality*

The first and most important point, then, is the absolute necessity to recognize the moral dimension of the Common Good, to which every other dimension is ordered. The Common Good is, naturally, a "good," a "good" for the person as such (practical, not technical) and thus a moral good. One of the authors who has recently vindicated the inevitability of the moral dimension in human agency is Charles Taylor. Commenting on his work, Daniel M. Weinstock says: "One of Taylor's main achievements was to discredit the view of human agency according to which action can be understood solely in terms of the agent's preferences and of his efforts to satisfy these preferences; and to suggest the greater plausibility emphasizing the agent's second-order reflection upon such preferences, and the evaluative frameworks which make such second-order reasoning possible."[33]

This moral dimension, denied or ignored by deism, naturalism and the dominant modern systems of thought,[34] consists of acknowledging and legitimating the space defined by distinctions of worth within which a full agent exists. Full agency, full "personhood," requires this moral horizon to define an individual's identity: "our self-understanding essentially incorporates our seeing ourselves against a background of what I have called 'strong evaluation,'"[35] adds Charles Taylor. The "strong eval-

[33]Daniel Weinstock, "The Political Theory of Strong Evaluation", in J. Tully (ed.), *Philosophy in the Age of Pluralism: The Philosophy of Charles Taylor in Question*, Cambridge University Press, 1994, p.171.

[34]Cf. C. Taylor, *Sources of the Self*, p.382. Taylor says that deism and naturalism lack a proper moral dimension, are one-dimensional and leave no place to what makes life significant; they are only focused on a desire-fulfillment dynamic. Moreover, and despite the dangers of generalizations, I here understand by "denial of the moral dimension" either reductionism or dualism, viz. to explain the moral dimension in physical terms or to completely separate it from the physical world. These two interpretations distort the essence of the moral dimension, and the major philosophical systems of Modernity have one flaw or the other.

[35]C. Taylor, "Introduction", in *Philosophy and the Human Sciences*, p.3.

uation" consists in admitting that there are things with a higher, categorical or unconditioned importance or worth, and other things that are not so important. In other words, recognizing that we experience *real* distinctions of worth, instead of the uniformity or the leveling of value (equivalent to no value at all) proclaimed by different kinds of materialism and other modern systems.

This moral dimension, then, is constitutive of human agency, namely, of being a person. The reason for this, as Taylor also clarifies in *Sources of the Self*, is that there is an essential link between personal identity and moral orientation: "to know who you are is to be oriented in moral space."[36] A person experiences him/herself as a person only through his/her specific reference to the good; a person knows who he/she is by knowing what are the valuable things for him/her.

Furthermore, the moral dimension of existence is an inevitable fact of experience; there is no sense in trying to deny it. Even doctrines that intend to stand without it, or to despise it as a subjective projection or things alike (materialism, hedonism, naturalism, some kinds of liberalism), make moral claims. It is not possible to make this sort of claim without making moral distinctions, which implies, in its turn, some kind of strong evaluation and qualitative distinction.[37] Therefore, these doctrines also have their specific moral framework determining their judgements, even if they do not recognize it explicitly. And this is not necessarily a matter of bad will. Many defenders of these doctrines believe in their discourse of moral neutrality, not knowing that their judgements inevitably presuppose a moral standpoint that may be unconsciously determining them.

Undoubtedly, through theoretical exercise and seeking specific theoretical goals, it is possible and sometimes even convenient to abstract and leave aside for a moment the moral dimension of the human being. Nonetheless, taking this as a norm and affirming the resulting image as reality cannot be responsible science, although it is exactly what modern epistemologies—based on the Natural Sciences' paradigm—always do: they set a priori conditions to their reasoning and discredit, a priori, the moral dimension of reality.

[36]C. Taylor, *Sources of the Self*, p.28.
[37]C. Taylor, *Sources of the Self*, p.332.

In addition, once we recognize the moral dimension in human nature, it is no longer unintelligible or naïve to affirm that the end of Politics is *virtue*, i.e. the complete development of human potentialities, as Aristotle and Thomas Aquinas said. Naturally this goal should not be understood in an univocal and dogmatic way, but rather must be articulated and presented in a plausible way, respecting different moral views, cultural backgrounds, etc. Yet, to qualify a *telos*, adapting it to the specific circumstances of each community and making it practical is not to reject it. On the contrary, because it is a matter of practical reason this end can take indefinite shapes as long as it maintains its intrinsic and constitutive form: the reference to the good of the person.[38] Just as the good life of a person, theoretical or political, can be achieved and materialized in diverse manners, according to the subject and the circumstances, the Common Good is also concretized in one particular form in each community. Universality of the first principles of practical reason and of natural law is applied in diverse ways regarding the contingencies of each situation. This idea will be clearer after explaining some peculiar features of practical knowledge in the next section.

II.2 *Plausibility*

A second essential characteristic of practical reason that should be acknowledged for a better understanding of the Common Good is its mode of reaching truth. As it was already said, "truth" in this way of thinking (i.e. to know which is the best action in order to achieve the good of the person) is reached by means different than in theoretical or technical thinking, and except for some general margins, it is impossible to predict results.[39] G.E.M. Anscombe puts it clearly: "The problems that would be raised in an attempt to draw a boundary line (or a boundary area) here are obviously complicated. And while there are certainly some general remarks that ought to be made (here), and some boundaries that can be drawn, the decision on particular cases would for the most part be

[38]Cf. J. Maritain, p.93.

[39]In *Sum. theol. i-ii ad 3,* Aquinas says that truth is not the same for the practical as for the speculative intellect. And the reason he gives is that in speculative thinking truth is conformity between the intellect and the thing, while in practical thinking truth is conformity with the right appetite.

determined "according to what's reasonable" (…) and for this there can *in principle* be no canon other than giving a few examples."[40] Anscombe highlights the difference between "law" understood in modern terms, i.e. univocal, necessary and uniformly applied; and "norm" understood in the Aristotelian sense of "model," of acting as the prudent man would do and choosing whatever is reasonable according to the infinite possible circumstances.

Nonetheless, prudence, the specific virtue and articulator of practical reasoning, is not intelligible, obscure and almost unconceivable to Modern mechanistic and idealistic mind. Law is only the premise of practical judgement. It is rational, universal and necessary, but between it and the particular action there will be always a space to be filled by decisions that cannot be contained in laws, for they are not general. This gap is filled by prudence. The last conclusion of practical reasoning, which is an action, is more determined by inclination than by reason. It is not logically connected to the first principles; its truth is rather the work of affective connaturality.

Inclination, on the other hand, is not arbitrariness. It is not demonstrative knowledge, but it is indeed knowledge. When inclinations are sound, the judgements asserted with them are perfectly certain in their own way. "In fact, this is the only way to ascertain practical judgements when they are considered concretely."[41] In other words, when moral and political problems are considered in all their concreteness and individuality, the last word belongs always to sound inclination. Furthermore, "knowledge by inclination is not clear; it may be certain but it is not clear. In fact, it is incommunicable."[42]

This kind of knowledge does not exclude rational evidence, but precedes it. Even in theoretical sciences there is knowledge by inclination, some "intuition of the solution" in the mind of the well-trained scientist before he is able to demonstrate it through logical connections from the first principles. In practical matters there is no possibility of complete logical demonstration (because they involve reference to all the contingencies of the particular situation), but there are inclinations that may be

[40] G. E. M. Anscombe, p.191.

[41] I. Simon, p.128.

[42] I. Simon, p.129.

sound, and should try to be rationalized as much as possible acknowledging that they will never be completely clear. This will be "enlightened prudence." How can we know, then? Anscombe already said it: "according to what is reasonable," which is the same as to judge like "the honest conscience of a man trained in justice," the prudent man.

Consequently, "enlightened prudence" will be the ultimate criterion to know practical truth. This notion, however, is obscure to the Modern mind. Charles Taylor turns up the coin showing that what on the side of the agent is prudence, on the side of the evaluator is plausibility. And this, again, is perfectly rational. In *Sources of the Self*, Charles Taylor characterizes and legitimates this different way to reach and recognize truth. He says that in matters of practical reasoning, "the measure of reality in human affairs is that which after critical reflection makes the best sense of our lives."[43] And he adds that this "making sense" must include all those "indispensable terms" for people's self-understanding of their lives, where moral qualities have a central place. Consequently, "truth" in practical reason is a matter of plausibility, of making sense. Rationality is no less a matter of plausibility than logical consistency. And thus, to be rational in the pursuit of the Common Good is not to mechanically follow laws deduced from general principles or to be able to exhaust its content in a descriptive list of goods. Further, the particular political decisions will not be refuted through the evidences of Natural Sciences, but instead the criterion will be "reasonableness."[44] To expect any other kind of argument in practical reason is to fail to identify the *kind of object* reason is considering, for in this area the relation between the master ideal and the discrete norms may be quite complex.

In Ethics, and thus also in Politics, there is not only one single correct answer, one single way of realizing the Good. Contrariwise, as there are several partial goods, each of them better than the rest in some aspect, there will usually be many possibilities of correct decisions, a set of incommensurable "correct choices" distinguished by the aspect of the good that is outranked. This partiality in the realization of the good in human action is the ultimate explanation for the absence of absolute

[43]C. Taylor, *Sources of the Self*, p.57.

[44]Naturally, sometimes being "reasonable" asks for Natural Sciences' evidences.

answers in practical reason,[45] because there will always be several possible ways of achieving the end, each of them better "in some sense." Therefore, enlightened prudence becomes the qualified criterion to choose the course of action, and plausibility the best way of verifying its practical truth.

II.3 *Teleology*

Finally, the third formally constitutive element of the Common Good that I want to highlight is teleology. When the essence and the existence of some entity are not identical—viz. the perfect tree and this particular tree or, in an analogical sense, the perfect society and the current society—we can assume that the actions or operations of that entity are directed towards progressively reaching that perfection. Obviously this statement contains many presuppositions that may not be admitted by the Modern mind, particularly the notion of "essence." However, there is another way of "showing" the truth of teleology even when it is theoretically denied: this way is through the notion of function. Ives Simon says: "What does 'it works' mean? It means something, it makes sense, if there is a set goal, an agreed end; working is the most obviously teleological thing in the world ... Without such initial setting of ends the notion of working is purely and simply nonsensical."[46] Even Hume, who through his sharp division of facts and values tried to completely discredit teleology and natural law, designed a "functional" ethics: an ethics justified as far as "it works," and "it works" because it directs human action to a previously (somehow) known end. According to Simon, one of the most profound reasons for the denial of teleology during Modernity has been the mathematization of sciences, for in Mathematics there are neither natures nor final causes.[47] However, despite the enormous utility of Mathematics in scientific inquiries, it is not reasonable to confuse the character of an instrument (however brilliant it may be) with the character of the object studied.

[45]Except for some Absolute Prohibitions, cf. Aristotle, *Ethica Nicomachea*, Book II, 6 (1107a8-13).

[46]I. Simon, pp.114-115.

[47]Cf. I. Simon, p.47.

Moreover, another "modern resistance" to the notion of teleology is to believe that it means determinism. Isaiah Berlin, sustaining this position, says: "I believe that purposes are imposed by human beings upon nature and the world, rather than pursued by them as part of their own central nature and essences (...) I believe that it is human beings (...) that form the world (in a way) which cannot be causally predicted. It is not part of a determinist structure, it does not march inexorably towards some single predestined goal."[48] Clearly this conception misunderstands practical reason. Teleology means to be inclined to the good, to be attracted by the good which is the realization of our own selves in the most perfect way. But there is no determinism in this process, as is shown by two simple reasons. The first is contingency. Since there is a plurality of causes at work in the world, they may easily interfere with each other, and a contingent event may take place at that point of interference. If the principle of causality is real, contingency might be equally real in the physical and the moral world. Furthermore, regarding human beings natural law operates in a peculiar way, for it exists as a rule inherent in the nature of things which does not direct operation in a determinate fashion, but governs behavior through judgement and through free choice.[49]

Consequently, the human—personal and social—process of self-realization may actually fail, either because we don't choose a "correct" good (a real, perfective good) among the options, or because we don't reach the chosen good due to different contingencies. Therefore this is not a deterministic structure, an unavoidable path. And since the effective realization of the good may take infinite different forms, there is no sense trying to find any "single predestined goal."

Another misunderstanding about teleology is to believe that a conscious promotion of the good (to orient the actions towards a desired end) is something different, something external and strange to the promotion of people's good and interests. Yet, on the contrary, teleology means to be inclined to the good, not an abstract good but the good of the person, an immanent good. This "good of the person," as it was above said, is obviously his/her happiness (*eudaimonia*), and thus his/her main objective

[48]I. Berlin, "Introduction" in Tully, J., p.2.
[49]Cf. I. Simon, p.122.

interest. Consequently, the promotion of the Common Good is, at least, the same as the promotion of the good (the complete development) of the people who constitute society, for the legitimate Common Good is immanent in man and calls for a constant distribution to the persons in whom society exists. The Common Good is not a work of art, achievable through *poiesis*, nor the greatest good to the greatest number. These two modern views misunderstand the essence of the Common Good which is, regarding the temporal society, the end of the moral virtues.[50] In other words, as much as the natural law is immanent in a person by reason of his being a being, by reason of his being an animal, and by reason of his being a rational agent with inclinations and tendencies that cannot be arbitrarily chosen; the Common Good, which is the end of these inclinations, is immanent to the person too.

In sum, if we accept the existence of a moral dimension in life, we must incorporate the concept of "good" to our judgements. This concept, in turn, imposes to reason another way of processing information, with different criteria for decision-making (enlightened prudence) and for verification (plausibility), along with another way of understanding the dynamic of social and personal life (teleology). These three notions, each in its level, have been excluded from modern political philosophy. The cause may be found in the evolution and history of ideas, but the most important fact is that this exclusion has not led to any happy result. The re-incorporation of these notions, then, or at least their re-consideration, seems a recommendable new scientific step for political theory.

III. ELEMENTS OF THE COMMON GOOD

Even though it is not possible to list the elements of the Common Good in such a way that their sum would be equivalent to the Common Good, just as the sum of virtues does not result in "happiness," it is nonetheless possible to identify some indispensable features of it. These features have different natures, and that may be a problem to fully visualize/understand the concept of Common Good. However, when these elements are adequately coordinated, the notion becomes credible and operative. The specific features of the Common Good I want to point

[50]Cf. I. Simon, pp.105-106.

out here are: its material conditions, its dynamic aspects, and its essential point of view.

III.1 *Material conditions*

By material conditions I don't necessarily mean "physical" but rather "content of the Common Good". These conditions are not the Common Good itself but they facilitate its achievement. Traditionally, these components of the Common Good are said to be peace, order, freedom and justice. However, different authors have created different lists for these necessary or minimal elements. Maritain specifies more: he includes in his list the public goods (commodities and services, including infrastructure, laws and culture), sociological integration of all civic conscience, political virtues, sense of right and liberty, moral rectitude, justice, friendship, virtue and happiness in the individual lives of its members.[51] Despite its length, this list is not exhaustive and can never be exhaustive given the nature of the Common Good. Saint Thomas Aquinas is much more synthetic in his list. In *On Kingship* he says that the three necessary conditions for living well are: sufficient supply of things, unity of peace, and to be directed to acting well.[52] So then, summarizing these conditions, it may be said that the "material conditions" for the Common Good are the necessary material supply and a legal-cultural framework committed to defend and respect each *person qua person*, acknowledging and empowering the complete development of his/her potentialities.

The danger of listing conditions is to confuse the Common Good with these conditions, and thus treat it like a product, a work of art. This false identification nullifies the nature of the Common Good, and transforms it in an external/partial good, something similar to what Modern political theories understand by it. Saint Thomas Aquinas has a penetrating passage showing that techniques and technical goods are conditions but not the Common Good itself. "If such an ultimate end either of an individual man or a multitude were a corporeal one, namely, life and health of the body, to govern would then be a physician's charge. If that ultimate end were an abundance of wealth, then knowledge of economics would have

[51]Cf. J. Maritain, p.42.

[52]T. Aquinas, *On Kingship*, translated by G. B. Phelan, The Pontifical Institute of Medieval Studies, Toronto, 1949, IV, 118.

the last word in community's government."[53] Health and wealth are conditions; they are not the Common Good.

III.2 *Dynamic aspects*

What I call "dynamic aspects" are not just conditions but rather, on the one hand, manifestations or signs of the Common Good, and on the other, essential constituents of the "good activity" or "good operation" of society. Concretely, I want to point out what Jacques Maritain called the "two laws of the Common Good"[54]—the law of redistribution and the law of transcendence—along with deliberation. The first law indicates that the good of the whole flows back to the persons. This redistribution applies to material and non-material goods, although the non-material goods are the most important because, while "participation" of material goods is division of the valuable thing, "participation" of non-material goods (like virtue, membership, love, etc.) binds people together and forms community. Ives Simon stresses the idea that a good is common if and only if it is of such nature as to call for common pursuit and common enjoyment. Therefore, among these goods, we find things as different as public safety, treasures of knowledge, and above all, "the constant action, silent most of the time, by which society maintains in each of us some clarity of moral conscience, some willingness to prefer right to wrong, and some comforting energy against the forces of desperation."[55] It is important to notice that the Common Good comprehends outward goods (prosperity, safety) as much as inward goods (culture, morality), but *if these are not distributed they lose their character of Common Good.*

Maritain's second law is the law of transcendence, and it refers to the public recognition of the value of personal transcendence.[56] This does not mean any kind of fundamentalism or religious state, or even ignoring jurisdictional spheres of different kind of laws. However, it does mean the acknowledgement of this important dimension in human beings, and the fostering of its personal and communal development. Finally, I add to Maritain's two laws the continuous process of deliberation that shall char-

[53]T. Aquinas, *On Kingship*, 106.

[54]J. Maritain, pp.66-67.

[55]Cf. I. Simon, p.91.

[56]Cf. J. Maritain, p.67.

acterize a society realizing its Common Good, which is also a manifestation of the dynamism of social *eudaimonia.*

Furthermore, these three dynamic features reflect two very important aspects of the Common Good. First, they evidence that "social *eudaimonia*" is an activity, just as personal *eudaimonia*, for it can never be "completely completed." There is no chance for an "end of history." Second, these features clearly reveal that the realization of the Common Good is an activity of practical reason. For instance, the law of redistribution is the social equivalent to self-reference of the will in individual action, through which people acquire good or bad habits. *Praxis*, as it was stated at the beginning, is essentially reflexive. The law of transcendence, on the other hand, refers to the constitutive relation to the absolute good that defines human identity. Finally, deliberation expresses the continuous process through which the particular goods are achieved, the "enlightened prudence" that may never be replaced by general laws.

III.3 *Point of view*

Besides the "material content" and dynamic aspects that may be identified in the Common Good, the most important is to acknowledge its intrinsic point of view. This new focus marks the main differences from our traditional political visions, and although at first sight it might seem utopian or naïve to our excessively technified reason, it is interesting to explore the new horizon it opens. The point of view from which the Common Good shall be seen is a moral point of view. And this reintroduction of the moral dimension in political deliberation would be absolutely determinant to social organization. Another way of saying the same, yet avoiding the term "moral" that may cause resistance in some modern circles, is to speak about the reintroduction of the *person qua person* as the subject and object of deliberation, with his/her inviolable dignity and absolute value.

Naturally, no "technical ethics"—like Consequentialism, that seeks the most efficient means to achieve the best "product"[57]—or "technical politics"—like Socialism or Liberalism, that seek the maximization of a particular good and consider only the "material individual"[58]—can give

[57]See A. Carrasco, *Consecuencialismo. Por que no*, Eunsa, 1999.

[58]See J. Maritain, *Person and Common Good*, chapter V.

an account of the moral dimension. Consequently, they are not able to give an account of the human *person qua person* either, because, as Karol Wojtyla expresses in his collection of essays *Person and Community*,[59] personal fulfillment depends heavily in the social process and the conditions for social relations. These conditions are only met when citizens are considered in all their dimensions, i.e. as "persons" rather than as "individuals,"[60] and are radically oriented to the "absolute good" rather than to some particular technical good. In other words, the possibility of personal fulfillment requires the reintroduction of moral dimension in the political horizon and requires that the Common Good—understood as the basic concept of social practical reasoning—returns to the axial position in our political deliberation.

IV. CONCLUSION

Obviously, the above statement cannot mean that Politics should completely abandon technical reason. There are several kinds of problems, especially in mass societies, which can only be technically solved. Political ability requires several arts or techniques to reach its goal, but it needs them as instruments. No art can solve any problem of human use by itself; it is human prudence, informed by the first principles of practical reason, the one that can do a humanly good or wrong use of those arts. Techniques or arts, then, are indispensable. However, the objective individual—the anonymous, exchangeable, material fraction of society, the object of Economics and Statistics—is not the whole person. That individual *is* a real object and many times must be considered in that objective (technical) way, but not *always*, for that is not the whole reality. The

[59]"The social process, which ought to lead to the genuine subjectivity of all, is then checked or even reversed, because human beings cannot find themselves as subjects in this process. Social life goes on as though beyond them—not so much in opposition to them but rather "at their expense." They, in turn, although existing and even acting together with others, do not fulfill themselves in this life, even because they have estranged themselves or because society, through some faulty structure, does not give them a basis for self-fulfillment or even denies them the rights needed to it." K. Wojtyla, "The person: subject and community," in *Person and Community*, p.256.

[60]Cf. J. Maritain.

anonymous statistic individual is also a person, a totality of meaning, an end in himself, who cannot be captured by technical reason and is not measured by efficiency. An economist qua economist is not a good statesman, because the good government of society essentially differs from the good management of a big company. The virtues or the skills needed are different for each case, since the ends of these practices are different and irreducible: one is efficiency and the other is the Common Good.

The specific feature picked up in the notion of Common Good is "personhood." The Common Good is not only the perfection of external actions but, above all, the perfection of the hearts of men. The reason for this is the particular reality of which social and political life is made, namely, "persons." Consequently, the successful cooperation of men in the performance of collective transitive actions is one aspect of the Common Good; but there are immanent actions which, because of the awareness of unity they bring, assume a social character. Clearly these communions are the most genuine and most profound of all social facts, and the good condition of these communions, the good condition of whatever pertains to acting together in these immanent actions, is the deepest and the most precious part of the Common Good.[61] Since the most important part of community life takes place in the heart of man, the Common Good is essentially a moral good.

Therefore, the reconciliation of these two constitutive dimensions of men, and the correct use of each mode of reason, is the task of practical or political wisdom, namely, of the virtue of prudence. While the touchstone for technical reason is efficiency, the touchstone for practical reason is dignity. And in a political scheme led by the Common Good, in case of conflict, dignity must take primacy over efficiency.

Is this utopian? As much as it is utopian to intend to live a good life, to believe in the possibility of human self-realization, to direct our personal life towards *eudaimonia*. Modern paradigms of knowledge, which have obscured our comprehension of practical reason, will discourage this path. However, with the reintroduction of the moral dimension in political deliberation, we may be able to "see" again the end, the telos, of society, and that may be a good start toward recuperating the "person"

[61]Cf. I. Simon, pp.95-96.

after centuries of reductive Modernity. "For natural law exists implicit in the natures of men individually and collectively. Natural law is like an axiom of geometry in one sense. It cannot be repealed, but it can be ignored."[62]

[62]Harvey Wheeler, "Natural Law and Human Culture", in John Cogley et al.: *Natural Law and Modern Society*, The World Publishing Company, Ohio, 1963, p.200.

REPORTS

ANNUAL INTERNATIONAL MEETING OF THE AMERICAN MARITAIN ASSOCIATION

Critical aspects of our nature as humans will be overlooked if we do not reflect upon how we know things. In many ways the postmodern world understands human knowing only in part and then mistakes that part for the whole (even though that part may be different for each of the various philosophical traditions). Now if it is true that many of our major important decisions and actions are based upon, and are limited to, the parameters of what we think we can know, then these errors can have serious consequences. That, in essence, was what the Annual International Meeting of the American Maritain Association on "Maritain, Gilson, and the Many Ways of Knowing," was all about. While the conference had many topic areas ranging from education to architecture, we can briefly touch upon four of them: understanding the nature of the intellect, the nature of its objects, its nature as free, and its relationship to our culture.

Joseph M. Magee from the University of St. Thomas, spoke on "Aristotle and Aquinas on Proving the Intellect's Immateriality." I will try to paraphrase his argument. If the human mind is capable of knowing all things, this means that the intellect is not affected materially in the knowing process. Material change would limit this ability. Now all material things do get materially affected when they undergo a change. Therefore, no completely material thing can know. The senses *as such* are limited to one kind of object. Magee's talk pointed to the fact that when we do know, we do so by something that is immaterial; and this, of course, points to the unique nature of our knowing and how knowing really involves a "becoming" of the other, and this has tremendous implications.

The idea that the objects of human knowing are real entities outside the human mind, that a realist epistemology is critical, was found in many of the presentations. Some that might be cited are W. Matthews Grant's (Fordham University) "MacIntyre's Interpretation of an *adequatio intellectus et rei*," John F. X. Knasas's (Center for Thomistic Studies) "Transcendental Thomist Methodology and Maritain's 'Critical Realism,'" Peter Redpath's (St John's University) "Philosophy's Non-Systematic Nature: Maurer's Reflections on Aquinas' Notion of the Unity of the Sciences," Brendan Sweetman's (Rockhurst

University) "The Postmodern Turn: Language and Myth in Roland Barthes," and Raymond Dennehy's (University of San Francisco) "The Loss of the Knowing Subject in Contemporary Epistemology." If we do not know real things in the world, all knowing is but a branch of psychology.

We know real objects outside of the mind, but the way we know them differs depending upon the kind of knowledge we are employing. Discussing Maritain's notions of theoretical, practical, and connatural knowledge, and aligning them with the transcendentals, I in my "Knowing Our Knowings" argued that in order to avoid confusion, it is critical to identify the different kinds of knowledge that we use, and also, to recognize their blind spots.

A realist philosophy is also critical to the understanding of freedom. A paper that gave great insights here was Francis Slade's (St. Francis College) "Subjection or Subordination? Two Views of Rule and of Knowledge in Political Philosophy." Slade argued that epistemology was not the ruler of philosophy. Descartes was wrong. Without a realist epistemology, there can be no real theoretical or practical knowledge. For the ancient and medieval mind, freedom was a possibility, for the modern Cartesian mind, it is a necessity and directionless. For the modern mind, all ends are reduced to mere purposes, and thus are limited to simply a "psychological" reality. For the modern mind there is no teleology and no direction. This is an amazing point! Where are we going with our knowledge? With a modern mind set, can we ever become freer?

Also notable with regard to freedom was Henk E. S. Woldring's (Free University, Amsterdam) "Understanding Freedom as a Way of Knowing Social Life." "Are we governed by physical laws alone or not?" Not if we have free-will. Maritain admits there are instincts, tendencies, but freedom transcends these. And if freedom exists in the individual it should also apply to the state; and it is public spirit, service, justice, and care which are at the base of freedom and give freedom its strength.

Many underestimate the effects of our culture upon our minds and upon those of our children. John Trapani, Jr. (Walsh University) in his "The Air We Breathe: Our Knowledge of Reality and the Reality of Our Knowledge" gave a very provocative paper that still resonates in my head (I have four children) many months after the conference. "If you were in a crowded smoke-filled room, you can't come away not smelling of smoke!" So too, there often is an uncritical absorption of our culture. If the foods that we eat and the air that we breathe improve our physical health, then surely the cultural environment is critical to the soul's health as well. Think of our knowledge. The knower becomes one with the object known. Pure sensation is a myth. It is always an "I" that knows, and an "I" that perceives. Cultural forces become a part of us by cognitive necessity. If one thinks about the fact that the intellect will not search out further than the imagination will allow it to go, then the proper education of the imagination is critical.

If culture affects the soul and character, then *a fortiori*, it must affect our religious life. Steven Schloeder, (Dominican School of Philosophy and Theology) in his "Recovery of the Symbolic" argued that architecture should respect the whole person. So much of current religious architecture is banal and reflective of the enlightenment. It is reductionistic and based upon function alone. A Thomistic examination of human knowledge reveals that we first apprehend things through sense organs and then form a phantasm in the *imaginarium* in which there is an emotional charge. There is no knowing of concepts without recourse to the phantasm. There is no image-less knowledge; and if Church architecture is abstract, it frustrates this very experience. It short-circuits full human participation in religious devotion. The mind naturally seeks knowledge about essences and gets rest. But if Church architecture is abstract, the mind immediately rests, and so loses interest. Church interiors need to inflame our *imaginarium*. They must seek to engage the whole person, soul and body, intellect and senses.

Ultimately, it seems that if we are more consciously aware of how we as humans know things, then we will be more careful of what "comes" into our minds with regard to harmful influences and also be more careful to artfully structure the images of those most important things so that the corresponding realities *do* "come inside" well. In short, to put it in a rather crass way, we should avoid those things that are interesting but harmful, and avoid making symbols of those realities that are important, dull.

Finally, the religious dimension of culture is critical. One primary reason for rejecting God in our culture is the problem of evil. Douglas

Geivett, (Biola University) in his "A Problem of Evil for Naturalists"—echoing C.S. Lewis—presented a wonderful counterattack to the naturalist who argues from the problem of evil. Define it! Define "evil." Force the one with the problem to define the word and give the extension of the term in a meaningful way; and to do so without using the notion of "ought" and implying a non-physical notion of "nature."

In sum, know how you know and you will be enabled to make that most important part of you, your intellect, as well as the whole person it governs thrive! Articles from this conference will be published by the American Maritain Association through the Catholic University Press of America. It will be entitled *Jacques Maritain and the Many Ways of Knowing* and it is edited by Professor Douglas A. Ollivant of the United States Military Academy at West Point.

Gregory J. Kerr
Allentown College of St. Francis de Sales

INTERFAITH DIALOGUE ON THE HUDSON RIVER WATERSHED

In the presence of the human, the natural world has no rights. We have a moral sense of suicide, homicide, and genocide, but no moral sense of biocide or geocide, the killing of the life systems themselves and even the killing of the Earth.[1]
(Thomas Berry)

For good reason is Tom Berry's observation frequently cited in the developing national discussion concerning the relationship between religion and the environment.

During the last thirty years environmentalism has taken hold of American life in ways that surpass even the civil rights, labor and women's movements. It has produced a vast body of law, hundreds of government agencies, and tens of thousands of lawyers, scientists, engineers, consultants, public officials and professional advocates who specialize in the analysis, development, and implementation or defeat of environmental policies.

But unlike most other American social movements, contemporary environmentalism has been molded less by an evolving moral debate than by reaction to crises. A necessary preoccupation with strange and unfamiliar issues such as pesticides that killed birds, rivers that burned and neighborhoods that were constructed atop toxic waste sites, seemed to leave little room for engaging a national debate over the rights of the natural world.

In the absence of that debate society at-large embraced environmental statutes as the basis for its values regarding nature and the environment. But with no foundation of normative moral principles the framers of those laws had based their statutes on a balancing act: What is the cost-

[1]Thomas Berry, *Ethics and Ecology*, Harvard Seminar on Environmental Values, Harvard University, April 9, 1996

benefit ratio of building a power plant versus protecting a fish species? How many cases of cancer should a legal chemical be allowed to produce

As a result, environmentalism has become trapped in a continuing negotiation over the administration of pollution laws that do not outlaw pollution, toxics laws that do not outlaw toxins and endangered species laws that do not outlaw the extinction of species. In short, there are no accepted norms of right and wrong when it comes to the American environment.

In an essay prepared for the milestone symposium "Spirit and Nature," held at Middlebury College in 1990, Steven Rockefeller, principle organizer of the symposium, wrote:

> What is needed is a commitment so wholehearted as to be justly termed religious in quality, to a new ecological worldview involving a dramatic transformation of the moral values and basic values that govern life in the industrial-technological world.
>
> Usually animals and ecosystems have been viewed primarily as means rather than as ends in themselves. They are thought to possess instrumental value but not intrinsic value. Consequently, a person's relation with them falls outside the sphere of right and wrong, unless these relations also affect the welfare of other persons. It is a widely shared outlook that is now being challenged, raising the possibility of a major revolution in the moral thinking of Western civilization.[2]

New York's Hudson River has long been a testing ground for new environmental initiatives. It is widely considered a birthplace of the modern environmental movement because of its hard won victory in the Storm King Mountain case for the right of a person to have standing in court to protect the environment. It is a fitting place, in the words of Reverend Jeff Golliher of the Cathedral of St. John the Divine, to "push the discussion past the place where it has settled."

The "Interfaith Dialogue on the Hudson River Valley" was formed by Professors John Cronin and Larry Hundersmarck of Pace University's Philosophy and Religious Studies Department and the Reverend Jeff Golliher to "establish spiritually derived moral principles for living in

[2]Steven C. Rockefeller, John C. Elder, eds. *Spirit and Nature*, Boston, Beacon Press, 1992

harmony with the Hudson River bioregion," according to the group's draft mission statement. The Dialogue is a group of fourteen individuals of diverse faiths, beliefs and disciplines that has met twice since the spring, 2000, and will be meeting again this autumn.

The impetus to organize the Dialogue came from the work of the Catholic Bishops of the northwest United States and Canada whose "Reflection in Preparation for a Pastoral Letter" about the Columbia River watershed was issued in the Spring of 1999. The Reflection wasted little time in addressing the matter of right and wrong on page two:

> Evils present periodically in the watershed include racism, sexism, classism and speciesism . . . These evils are expressed in individual sin when particular persons express these evils; communal sin when a community is permeated by them; and structural sin when social systems and institutions—political, economic, educational or religious—embody them.[3]

The members of the Dialogue have been unanimous that their starting point must be personal exploration—of each other's spirituality, ethical beliefs, and perceived need for the "revolution in moral thinking" of which Professor Rockefeller wrote. The meetings have been cause for interesting revelations among its members.

Andre Mele, Executive Director of Clearwater, a Hudson River environmental advocacy organization, said, "It was inspiring to take the time to reflect as a group on the principles that are the basis for our work. It is something that most of us don't take the time to do."

Katharine McLaughlin of the New York State League of Conservation Voters observed that, "Environmentalism is still an emerging value and there is an opportunity to define what it is but we need new words, a new language as well as a new morality."

Professor Gabe Gomes of Marymount College expressed what is per-

[3]Catholic Bishops of the Region, *The Columbia River Watershed: Realities and Possibilities—A Reflection in Preparation for a Pastoral Letter*, Columbia River Pastoral Letter Project, 1999

haps the group's greatest challenge: "We need a paradigm shift that recognizes the revelation of the divine in the earth."

John Cronin
Pace University

For more information regarding the *Interfaith Dialogue on the Hudson River Valley* contact John Cronin, 914-773-3692, JCronin@pace.edu.

Review Article

THE GOODNESS OF NATURE AND THE NATURE OF GOODNESS*

Kate Soper

One of the most persistently debated questions among environmental philosophers is whether nature has "intrinsic value," a topic upon which a great deal of academic literature is now available. Some of this has centered on the question as to what parts of nature may be said to have intrinsic value—whether we are to include the whole of being, biotic and abiotic, or restrict the claim to living beings, and if only the latter, whether intrinsic value is being ascribed to all living entities or only to the "higher" and more sentient among them. There has also been some discussion as to whether we are confining our claims about intrinsic value to planet earth, or extending them to all parts of the cosmos and to possible, and as yet unknown, forms of being within it.

But a major concern, also, has been with the quality of intrinsic value itself—with what is it that is being ascribed to nature, and on what basis, when it is said to have this kind of value. Some have argued that since values are dependent on human valuing, in claiming that nature has intrinsic value, we are asking no more than that human beings should value nature as an end in itself, and not simply because of its utility (or, as it is sometimes said, "instrumentally"). Such a view would deny that it makes sense to speak of nature having intrinsic worth in the absence of those who value it. Others, however, have quarreled with this "anthropocentric" approach on the grounds that, it treats the value of nature as merely a matter of subjective human appreciation, whereas in reality nature as such and "in itself" has objective value whether or not this is recognized and respected. Some, moreover, have insisted further that so far from nature's intrinsic value being dependent on human valuing, it is human beings themselves that detract from this value in intruding upon it

*K. Soper, (2000). "The Goodness of Nature and the Nature of Goodness." *Capitalism, Nature, Socialism*; 11(1). Reprinted with permission of Guilford Press.

or interacting with it. The intrinsic value of wilderness, for example, lies precisely in its being uncontaminated by any human intervention.

Now, it is not my purpose here to add further to these debates, or adjudicate over them, but rather to approach the issue of nature's intrinsic value from a slightly different angle by asking why those who advocate it are so keen to do so, and what difference they think it makes if we agree to their position. These questions may seem unduly naive. For are not their answers obvious? Those who insist on the intrinsic value of nature do so, it will be said, because this has too long been ignored, particularly by the industrialized Western societies, and only by arousing or restoring respect for the worth of nature as an end in itself, will these societies be encouraged to abandon their ecologically abusive policies.

Yet how far is this true? In other words, what bearing do our attitudes to nature, or our ontological conceptions of it, have on the way we treat it? Are changed perceptions of its worth always conducive to improved practice? Is the development of respect for nature's intrinsic value an essential precondition of such improvement? In any case, what counts as "improvement" in this area, and how far are what are deemed the correct forms of respect at any historical point in time conceived in the light of what is regarded at that time as ecologically desirable activity?

I submit that when unfolded along these lines, questions about the rationale for imputing intrinsic value to nature seem less naive than might at first appear, and the answers to them far from clear. Two books in particular have brought this home to me of late, both of them recently published; both of them dealing at length with questions relating to the value of non-human being, and both of them arriving at similar recommendations on our respect or care for nature, but on the basis of quite differing views about its intrinsic value.

In *Being and Worth*, Andrew Collier draws on aspects of the thought of Saint Augustine and Spinoza to argue that "being as being is good," and that everything which exists strives to remain in that condition, and to that degree possesses intrinsic value, and has a corresponding claim on our love.[1] Thus he quotes approvingly Augustine's claim (in *City of God*, book XII, chapter 5) that "all nature's substances are good, because they

[1]Andrew Collier, *Being and Worth* (London and New York: Routledge, 1999).

exist and therefore have their own mode and kind of being, and, in their fashion, a peace and harmony among themselves." Evil, it follows, is in some sense unreal: not being, but privation or lack of being, and is, according to Collier's Spinozist reading of Augustine, due to cognitive error, or failure of understanding of the being of the entity towards which the evil is being done. Thus it is argued, for example, that the more we know about non-human nature, both living and abiotic, the more we are likely to respect and love it, and that cruelty or vandalism towards other creatures or forms of being is largely a matter of cognitive deficiency rather than moral depravity.

Two points might be made here. One is that I suspect that Collier is inclined to overstate the role of cognitive knowledge, whether of animal ethnology, or of the physical, chemical and biological properties of nature, in arriving at the forms of appreciation we do have of non-human nature. It is certainly true that the knowledge we gain of other creatures influences our feelings about them, but it is equally true that our feelings inform our theories, and are always at work in our acceptance or rejection of them. (As Bolingbroke pointed out in response to Descartes' hypotheses about the machine-like nature of animals, "The plain man would persist in thinking there was a difference between the town bull and the parish clock.") We would have to acknowledge, moreover, that very often, as in the case of life-forms causing disease, more knowledge leads not to more love but simply to more efficient elimination.

But the other, and perhaps more important point, is that since Collier accepts not only Augustine's doctrine on the goodness of being, but also agrees with him in seeing beings and their worth as hierarchically ranked, with human beings at the top of the scale, and the least conspicuous and sentient beings at the bottom, not a great deal seems to be at stake here when it comes to possible changes in our actual policies towards nature. Irrespective of whether or not we accept the Augustinian line on the intrinsic value of all being (the claim, that is, that "being as being is good"), most of us will respect the being of human beings more than that of tigers, and that of tigers more than that of snails and that of snails more than that of viruses, and so on. What is more, most of our current dealings with non-human beings and entities are already based on observing a hierarchy of worth of this kind, and we readily justify the destruction of all sorts of forms of existence by reference to its rankings. Admittedly,

Collier, in effect, accepts this. Thus he writes, for example,

> It should be clear from the fact that non-human and even non-living entities are good in the sense that I am using the word, that this sense is not the same as moral goodness. It could be called a pre-moral good in that morality is based on it. Morality presupposes ontological good and consists in loving it in due order, and very largely - in fighting off threats to ontological good. Morality is for the most part the negation of the negation of ontological good. But moral good and evil may lead to an ordering of our sympathies, which is not the same as ontological ordering. For instance, I think it follows from this conception of the good that to take pleasure in killing an animal is very morally bad. In the light of this, consider the anti foxhunting slogan, "Which animal in a red coat has your sympathy?" In one sense, of course the fox does: if it is within one's power to do so, one should enable it to escape. Yet if you have to choose between giving essential help to a seriously injured fox or to a seriously injured foxhunter, you should without hesitation do the latter. This also follows from the ontological ordering of goods.[2]

Collier also readily admits that there are many other, and rather thornier, problems about the prioritization of entities in the ontological order, and would insist that he is concerned only with the general plausibility of the Augustinian ethic, and not with deriving detailed moral prescriptions from it.

Yet one must question how far the plausibility of any theory of the good can, in fact, be divorced from consideration of what moral guidance it can provide without it becoming philosophically redundant. In making this point, I should emphasize that my concern is not to defend a less "anthropocentric" approach than Collier's to non-human being. I am not, for example, inclined to dispute the rightness of sacrificing bacterial or viral life forms to the health of human beings. My point, rather, is that when it comes to our policies on the treatment of human illness, very little, if anything, hangs on whether we think the being of any bacteria or viruses that may be causing the illness has some intrinsic value, or not. In either event we seek to destroy it, and have little problem in justifying our procedure. So although Collier clearly thinks that adopting the Augustinian line on the intrinsic value of non-human being will issue in more sensitive attitudes to animals and the natural environment, my sense

[2]Ibid. p.77.

is that our moral behavior towards other beings is less determined by our ontological commitments than he supposes.

It is interesting, moreover, in this connection to note that Tim Hayward in his recent book, *Political Theory and Ethical Values*, arrives at a position very close to that of Collier in the claims he makes about the importance of human respect and care for other creatures, but does so on the basis of rejecting any account in terms of the intrinsic value of non-human nature as a mistaken "dogma of ecologism." For Hayward, by contrast, the motives for looking after the abiotic environment can be derived from enlightened self-interest, and "the claim that beings other than humans are morally considerable can be stated and defended in its own terms, without any reference to intrinsic value."[3] Hayward, in fact, takes what seems to be an even stronger line on our duties towards other living beings than does Collier, arguing that humans not only have an interest in promoting ecological values, but a moral obligation to give "wholehearted respect" (i.e., an active respect which includes care) to non-human beings. But the grounds for this obligation lie not in the intrinsic value of either humans or non-humans, but rather in the fact (as Hayward seeks to persuade us) that there is no reason to have more reverence for human "rational nature" than for any other aspect of nature.

Yet this, too, is a difficult position to accept, in part because it must meet all the usual objections concerning the non-reciprocal nature of the imputed obligations (can we be morally obliged to respect and care for the bodily integrity of those who have no such respect for us or other species in nature?). But it is problematic in part, too, because in undermining the normal basis of our hierarchical ranking of species it leaves us with even less specific moral guidance on the issue of prioritization of species than does the position adopted by Collier. For how much care should we show, and to what beings, and for how long? Hayward seems to imply that "wholehearted respect" is due to all beings which can be viewed as having interests or a "good" of their own. Yet this could be theoretically construed to include all biotic entities, both animal and vegetable, the ivy no less than the oak, the green fly no less the rose, the

[3]Tim Hayward, *Political Theory and Ecological Values* (Cambridge: Polity Press, 1998), p.21.

mouse no less the lion or the dolphin. Clearly, in practice, there must be limits on the creatures or beings of nature towards whom human beings might be said to have special duties of care, and what can set these if not our intuitions and knowledge about the degree of approximation of other species to the forms of sentience, cognition and rationality we associate with our own?

In the end, then, sympathetic as I am to both Collier's and Hayward's attempts to enhance human respect and care for non-human being, in neither case (though for differing reasons) does it seem that any very concrete proposals can be adduced from their respective ontological positions, either on the forms this care should take, or on the discriminations to be made in respect of its recipients. In this sense, as suggested earlier, I am yet to be convinced that what matters when it comes to practical policies on animal welfare and environmental preservation is whether we believe, as Collier does, in the intrinsic goodness of nature, or whether we dismiss, as does Hayward, all claims about intrinsic value as ecological dogma.

Book Reviews

PHILOSOPHY OF LAW: AN ENCYCLOPEDIA
Edited by Christopher B. Gray. New York: Garland Publishing, 1999

Reviewed by Kathryn Gray Shaughnessy
Department of Philosophy, Fordham University

Gray and Garland have delivered on their promise to provide a basic, broad-based, encyclopedic resource on the philosophy of law. This two-volume set (850 pages) includes entries covering prominent figures, movements and issues in philosophy of law. While the set boasts a variety of authors, each covering their field of expertise with individual voice, special care seems to have been taken to maintain integrity of content and structure: entries are reasonably even-handed; longer entries—which seem proportionally allotted to the relative breadth or import of the entry—are structured to "define" the entry, cover historical background, and elaborate on the status of current debate. Bibliographic material is enclosed at the end of entries, for easy reference and follow-up research.

Given the breadth of the encyclopedia, this review focuses on those entries which will be of special interest to our readers involved in Natural Law Studies.

Richard Brodeus covers Aristotle's legal philosophy clearly, but given space restraints there is little reference to the law's place within his larger philosophy. Brodeus' historical coverage of Aristotle's influence, his analysis of Aristotle on justice and equality, as well as his evaluation of Aristotle's place within modern paradigms, are especially helpful. He addresses modern questions on interpreting the universality of "natural law" and attempts to clarify these questions by emphasizing Aristotle's notions of "common good" and "principle of justice," over any appeal to universality and equality of reason.

Oscar J. Brown masterfully handles the entry on Thomas Aquinas, presenting Aquinas' theory of law with admirable brevity and clarity. After enumerating the purposes of law within the larger teleological philosophy of creation and salvation, Brown outlines the different kinds of law and explains their interrelations within Aquinas' hierarchical structure. Covering Divine Law, Natural Law, Law of Nations and Human Law, Brown's definitions and clarifications of interrelations make this an excellent encyclopedic overview of Thomistic Law Theory.

The selection on Natural Law, adroitly handled by Virginia Black, covers the history of natural law from its source in Aristotle to its modern adherents and critics. Black crystallizes the importance of natural law's divergence from positive law theory, highlighting and defining the former's relation to prudential reason, rights, nature, ethics and virtue. Tracing the history of Natural Law in Aristotle and Aquinas, Black emphasizes the importance of codified law's integral relation to reason, its placement within the "matrix of morality" and within an effective and just society. In outlining the historical waxing and waning of natural law, she neatly integrates current problems of semantics (e.g., in reference to such key terms as nature), and underscores the import of current debates on the moral force of unjust laws, the "is/ought gap," and natural law's connection with natural rights. In canvassing the current literature on Natural Law studies, Black notes the recent rise in virtue studies and the pragmatic turn of naturalist/positivist debates, especially as they revolve around human rights violations. She suggests that the latter will lend greater urgency to acknowledging more permanent grounds for justification of domestic and international law.

In the succeeding entry on Natural Rights, Frederic R. Kellogg takes up the discussion of the relation of natural rights to natural law, traces the development of apriori rights, and echoes the concern that international coercion and corruption must serve as the impetus to explore secure ground for rights outlined in the UN Declaration of Human Rights.

Rights, liberty and their relation to natural law are covered under several separate entries: *Fundamental rights* is covered by Samuel Freema, who traces its roots to the natural law tradition, defines fundamental rights in a helpful way—including definition of its criteria terms of non-over-rideability and unalienability—and is clear in pointing out the bases of modern debates: Promotion and maintenance of equality of basic rights, presumption of certain capacities of reason (to plan and control actions, to understand and comply with social and moral norms, etc.), and general disputes over which rights are properly called fundamental (e.g., economic rights—relating to land ownership, use and resources for production, including even minimum wealth levels; political participation rights; privacy and anti-discrimination).

Sheldon Wein covers *human rights*, defining them as the natural or moral rights which humans have by virtue of being human, regardless of the conventions of the society into which they are born. He emphasizes that the import of acknowledging these rights is that they are considered to be the minimum standards of state conduct towards citizens. Employing Nozick's term of rights as Social Trump: "human rights. . .impose side constraints on the way any society can go about its business in a morally legitimate manner." Since not all governments acknowledge these rights or have legal systems to ensure their protection, Wein underscores the practical problem of global justice and the attempts that have been made to ensure that human rights are also legally recognized rights. Most helpful for readers interested in international standards of human rights is the listing of international code agreements—international charters, covenants and declarations—and the bodies that have convened to serve as enforcers of these minimum codes of conduct. Because of his concern for global justice, Wein attempts to debunk the notion that "rights" are based on "western" notions of individual liberty and takes issue with those positivists who critique inalienable rights, by pointing out that as rational beings, we have reason for including inalienable rights within the concept of human rights in order to avoid allowing "evil governments to disingenuously claim that those whose rights they are violating have abandoned those rights."

The passage on liberty, ably covered by George G. Brenkert, clearly defines liberty in terms of negative and positive freedoms, giving definitions within the defining criteria, making this entry quite helpful. *Negative* freedom is freedom from coercion: in order to limit individual freedom, or to justify coercion from society—(1) necessary condition is violation of harm principle—significant harm is done to the nonconsenting; (2) offense to others—pornography, obscenity, desecration; (3) harm to self—seat belts, motorcycle helmets, legal paternalism; and (4) immorality of action—euthanasia, sodomy, exploitation/violence against children (although this latter criterion is argued by some to be an unjust limitation unless it violates one of the first three as well). *Positive* freedom—freedom for self-determination, self-development, determining one's own course of action—requires that in order for actions to be free, some qualities are necessary (e.g., rationality, knowledge, emotional control, good ends towards which development is directed). The passage ends in tracing relations between individual liberties and laws that foster positive freedom and protect negative freedoms.

Russell Schaefer Landau's handling of the entry on *Rights and liberties* is a bit more technical than other entries, but in conjunction with the complementary sections above, it helps to tease out relations between freedom and laws. He covers rights and liberties from the legal framework of Hohfeld, but indicates that this starting point can be effective for moral analysis as well. He distinguishes between kinds of rights in terms of advantaged and disadvantaged; the first two deal with specific duties or permissions, the second two deal with conditions under which duties are assigned. Landau is especially helpful in later sections where he deals with a number of topics in a helpful way: the subtlety of correlative rights and duties, the protection of interests vs. protection of autonomous choice as the basis of rights ascription, and scope and stringency of rights as the "heart" of rights conflict.

While many of the entries related to Natural Law refer to positivism and its critiques of the natural law position, it is unfortunate that the entry on Legal Positivism itself is a bit disappointing. Vittorio Villa's entry is nearly wholly consumed in the difficult task of definition. The reader is provided with a very detailed account of the difficulties in defining LP, and is given some idea as to why these difficulties are important in the philosophy of law. Having established that, he proffers the option of adopting a conceptual definition which entails outlining those assumptions undergirding "relevancy" within various legal positivist paradigms. He points out that the common assumptions of positive law theorists are that all laws are positive laws, and that all positive laws are "radically contingent human artifact from the point of view of production and of its evaluation and/or justification." He presents an argument that the conceptual definition underscores the mutually exclusive concepts of positive law and natural law, without implying the separation of law and morals. He also treats other problems of the separation thesis and the "value freedom principle," but then just re-affirms that conceptually, the difference between naturalists and positivists is the stance of objective versus relative justification of laws. On the whole, the entry is somewhat helpful—mainly for its references to sub-entries and prominent names within legal positivism—but this rather basic entry is so free of historical background and so laden with meta-jargon as to render it inaccessible to the relatively uninitiated reader.

Overall, the *Encyclopedia* is a worthwhile reference for many legal terms and for the entries on figures in the philosophy of law. Treatment of some issues—especially those which would be considered relatively controversial from the legal/philosophical standpoint—can be uneven. They are, for the most part, handled well from the legal perspective, but references to moral or philosophical perspectives vary drastically. (Sometimes there is no reference at all to any philosophy behind the law.) e.g., Euthanasia and Suicide is handled mostly in terms of legal definition where philosophy only handles the distinctions between the various types of euthanasia, while the entry *Abortion and Infanticide* talks about the legal history of abortion while also highlighting the "significant philosophical and moral implications" of conflicting rights and personhood. As a general reference tool, however, these volumes will serve the reader well.

DARWINIAN NATURAL RIGHT: THE BIOLOGICAL ETHICS OF HUMAN NATURE

By Larry Arnhart. Albany:
State University of New York Press, 1998

Reviewed by Victoria M. Wulf
CUNY, Staten Island

In his book *Darwinian Natural Right: The Biological Ethics of Human Nature*, Larry Arnhart attempts to blend Aristotelian political theory, Darwinian natural selection, and Humean moral theory into an ethical position he calls "Darwinian natural right." In chapter 1, "Darwinian natural right" is described in ten propositions. In these ten propositions, Arnhart describes an Aristotelian and Humean naturalistic ethics and attempts to ground this ethics in Darwin's theory of natural selection. According to "Darwinian natural right," human beings desire to lead the good life through the satisfaction of their desires. Pursuing the satisfaction of desires is an inherently social and political enterprise. While we are born with natural potentials and inclinations, the fulfillment of these potentials and inclinations toward good actions requires social learning and moral habituation. According to "Darwinian natural right," morality does not involve attaining an altruistic selflessness, but instead is a matter of cultivating the immediate sympathy and benevolence we have for ourselves and our families and extending this sympathy beyond the immediate familial range to the rest of society. On this view, our love for others is not an attempt at selflessness, but instead is an extension of our own self-love. Central to "Darwinian natural right" is that this inherently social view of ethics rooted in natural desire can be explained by an appeal to Darwinian natural selection.

Arnhart's "Darwinian natural right" is strongly influenced by Aristotelian ethics. Like Aristotle, Arnhart agrees that the starting point for human morality is a general account of the normative structure of animal movement. In the first of his ten propositions, Arnhart states, "the good is desirable, because all animals capable of voluntary movement pursue the satisfaction of their desires as guided by their information about the world" (pg. 6). With Aristotle, Arnhart also agrees that human beings are by nature social and political animals; that is, we have inborn natural potencies and inclinations that can be fulfilled only through a thoroughly social and political life. Chapter 3 presents a critique of the Hobbesian dichotomy between politics and nature. Rather than agreeing with Hobbes that politics is an artificial human construction and that "man is made fit for society not by nature but by education" (pg. 51), Arnhart agrees with Aristotle that human beings are naturally endowed with certain potentialities that can be fulfilled only through the political activities of learning and habituation.

The specifically Humean aspect of "Darwinian natural right" is found in Arnhart's claim that ethics is based in the development of what Hume calls the "moral sense". The "moral sense" can be defined as the natural social feelings of sympathy and benevolence that are necessary in order for any social cooperation to occur. These social feelings of sympathy and benevolence begin between family and friends but can be extended beyond family and friends to strangers. Such an extension of sympathy is one of the main tasks of ethical living. From these feelings of sympathy and benevolence, according to Hume, human beings attain a natural sense of right and wrong. While the "moral sense" is rooted firmly in these social feelings of sympathy and benevolence, Hume also insists that reason determines the truth and falsity of the judgments that accompany each passion. As Arnhart states of Hume's position, "Moral judgments are accurate when they correctly report what our moral sentiments would be in a given set of circumstances" (pg. 70). Moral judgments, for Hume, are not objective or universal in the sense that they are true independent of human beings, but rather "they are factual judgments about the species-type pattern of moral sentiments in specified circumstances" (pg. 70).

Arnhart's "Darwinian natural right" position is specifically Dar-winian in that Arnhart argues that this Aristotelian and Humean account of ethics can be grounded in or supported by natural selection. As Arnhart states, "Modern Darwinian biology supports this understanding of the ethical and social nature of human beings by showing how it could have arisen by natural selection through evolutionary history" (pg. 7). In *The Descent of Man*, Darwin claims that he will approach morality, not as a Kantian search for moral "oughts," but instead "exclusively from the side of natural history" (pg. 75). Since Darwin firmly believed that one of the central traits of the human species is the duration and intensity of child care, Darwin concurs with Aristotle and Hume that human beings must be inherently social animals. From the bonding between parents and children, Darwin believed that through habit and natural selection we extend our sympathies beyond our families to the rest of society. As Arnhart quotes Darwin, "The feeling of pleasure from society is probably an extension of the parental or filial affections, since the social instinct seems to be developed by the young remaining for a long time with their parents; and this extension may be attributed in part to habit, but chiefly to natural selection" (pg. 75). Darwin further gives a developmental account of morality as emerging through four stages. Arnhart states,

> First, *social instincts* would have led human ancestors to feel sympathy for others in their group, which would promote a tendency to mutual aid. Second, the development of *intellectual faculties* would allow early human ancestors to perceive the conflicts between instinctive desires, so that they could feel dissatisfaction at having yielded to a momentary strong desire (like fleeing from injury) in violation of some more enduring social instinct (like defending one's group). Third, the acquisition of *language* would permit the expression of social opinions about good and bad, just and unjust, so that primitive human beings would respond to praise and blame in satisfying their social instincts. Fourth, the capacity for *habit* would allow individual conduct to conform to social opinions through acquired dispositions. (pg. 76)

Given this account, Darwin agrees with Hume and to some extent Aristotle that the moral sense involves a development of our inborn instincts into social habits that are either encouraged or discouraged by our fellow human beings.

After explaining this evolutionary account of human moral development, Arnhart then argues that we can extract a normative set of twenty natural desires that are universal to all human societies. Arnhart states that these twenty natural desires "have evolved by natural selection over four million years of human evolutionary history to become components of the species-specific nature of human beings, that they are based in the physiological mechanisms of the brain, and that they direct and limit the social variability of human beings as adapted to diverse ecological circumstances" (pg. 36). These natural desires are universal, not because they are a set of universal abstract rules or even because they apply to a universal human essence, but instead because they are manifested as a universal pattern of desires across the same species throughout history.

Arnhart's appeal to a universal pattern is not an appeal to universal ethical principles, but instead is an appeal to universal historical norms. After four million years of human evolutionary history, the human species has developed twenty "general categories of desire" that have been manifest in diverse ways in all human societies. These twenty desires are listed as (1) A Complete Life (2) Parental Care (3) Sexual Identity (4) Sexual Mating (5) Familial Bonding (6) Friendship (7) Social Ranking (8) Justice as Reciprocity (9) Political Rule (10) War (11) Health (12) Beauty (13) Wealth (14) Speech (15) Practical Habituation (16) Practical Reasoning (17) Practical Arts (18) Aesthetic Pleasure (19) Religious Understanding and (20) Intellectual Understanding. These twenty desires constitute the universal standard from which social practices can be judged as either frustrating or fulfilling human desire.

Although Arnhart believes that these twenty natural desires constitute the universal standard from which we can judge social practices, he stresses that prudence is needed in judging the expression of each desire according to the particular conditions of each particular society. Arnhart states, "Judging human virtues and political regimes cannot be determined by universal rules because the diversity in the individual and social circumstances of life requires prudence or practical wisdom, which cannot be reduced to abstract rules" (pg. 2). Arnhart thus agrees with Aristotle that the human good is at once variable and universal. It is universal in that after 4 million years of evolution, the human species has developed twenty general categories of desire. It is variable in that the expressions of these desires will differ according to individual temperaments and particular societies.

Important for "Darwinian natural right" is the rejection of a strict separation between nature and nurture. Arnhart believes that our nature must be nurtured; that is, that our animal nature as human beings must be cultivated in order for us to become fully political and ethical animals. Arnhart writes, "In calling these twenty desires 'natural', I do not mean to imply that they arise spontaneously in all human beings without any cultivation by habit or learning. 'Nature' has many different meanings. I assume a complex conception of nature as both original potential and developing potential" (pg. 36). Instead of understanding human nature as something complete at birth apart from any habituation or learning, Arnhart claims that we are given inclination and potentials that need to be nurtured. Thus, our inborn animal inclinations give us the potential to lead a good life, but these inclinations need to be cultivated toward social cooperation if we are to attain the full development of our moral and political capabilities.

Consistent with his claim that nature must be nurtured, Arnhart also rejects a strict separation between nature and culture. Rather than understanding culture as an autonomous social construct that transcends human nature, Arnhart understands culture more broadly as "the flow of information (by social learning) between animals about their physical environment and their social relationships" (pg. 67). Our culture is rooted in our nature as social and political animals. Human culture differs from non-human culture only in the degree of complexity but not in kind. Because of our capacity to use language, human cultures are far more complex than other animal cultures.

The strength of Arnhart's book lies in his commitment to grounding ethics in empirical fact. He offers extensive biological evidence in support of the twenty natural desires. In chapter 2, by considering the life of the hermit crab and the honey bee, Arnhart gives extensive biological support for his Aristotelian claim that all animal movement has a normative structure rooted in desire. Also, chapter 5 is devoted exclusively to presenting biological evidence for the claim that parental care is a natural desire.

One weakness of Arnhart's book is that Arnhart fails to offer the reader a careful explanation of the theory of natural selection. Although Arnhart gives a thorough account of Darwin's evolutionary theory of morality, Arnhart fails to give the same thorough attention to Darwin's theory of natural selection. Central to the argument for "Darwinian natural right" is the claim that the twenty universal natural desires of the human species have evolved by natural selection over four million years. Yet, in *Darwinian Natural Right*, the reader is offered only the briefest explanation of natural selection in three sentences in the last five pages of the book (see pg. 269). Since so much of Arnhart's argument for "Darwinian natural right" rests on the theory of natural selection, a careful evaluation of this theory—from the viewpoint of contemporary biologists and philosophers of science—would have been helpful in strengthening Arnhart's thesis.

GETTING BACK INTO PLACE, TOWARD A RENEWED UNDERSTANDING OF THE PLACE-WORLD

By Edward S. Casey. Bloomington: Indiana University, 1993

Reviewed by John W.M. Krummel
Department of Philosophy, Belarmine College

In his book *Getting Back Into Place*, the American phenomenologist philosopher, Ed Casey expresses a renewed awareness of the importance of place in our ways of being and understanding. Casey's work is significant in that it makes explicit an understanding which has always already been in place but for the most part unexplicated in our intellectual theorizing. In his preface he writes that "[o]ur lives are so place-oriented and place-saturated that we cannot begin to comprehend, much less face up to, what sheer placelessness would be like"(p. ix). What Casey calls our "implacement" is taken as constitutive of our being. There is no being without place. But this importance of place as lived by our worldly existence has been too easily brushed aside by the modern philosophers to make room for the supposed primacy of measured space and time. One may also point out that a certain "crisis" of the contemporary technological age has resulted in a feeling of the loss of place, whether in relation to a longed-for "homeland" or in relation to Mother Nature, both violated for the sake of consumption; and further that this has allowed for the emergence, significant to our age, of the question of the problematic of place.

In the early modern age, with optimism science has hoped to grasp nature and world as purely accessible to rationality. This hope was expressed in the idealization of space and time as allowing for the purity of this measuring grasp. At the expense of meaningful place, the infinity of empty space was posited. But while Kant considered space and time to be forms of intuition, and internalized them as ideal, the environmental conditions exterior to the subject's mental space, the conditions of his pre-cognitive existential being were ignored. In the twentieth century, Heidegger's phenomenological-ontological critique of Kantian epistemology placed Kant's transcendental-ideal forms of space and time within the context of an extra-and pre-cognitive world as the non-ideal constituent of human existence (Dasein). Heidegger viewed the world as such, providing the horizon for human existence, as itself constituted by the temporality of our mortal existence. The world unfolds according to the way one existentially faces or approaches one's own temporal finitude. So both space and time as ideal forms of intuition along with the whole unfolding of being, in Heidegger's writings of the twenties, were traced to the ontologically deeper existential root of human existence: mortality. Some thinkers (like Buber, Nishida, and Watsuji) have criticized this seemingly one-sided focus upon time, to point out other synchronic structures which form human existence. However from the thirties on, Heidegger became increasingly concerned with the somewhat "spatial" (or better said, "placial") motifs of location, region, world, earth, dwelling and our current loss of place—ontological aspects which must be distinguished from space as measured and homogenous. The "temporocentrism" of his earlier works becomes loosened, and he comes to express the view that being can no longer be determined from mere temporality.

In the late twenties, right after the publication of *Being and Time*, a Japanese who attended Heidegger's lectures, Tetsuro Watsuji, criticized Heidegger for downplaying the importance of the environmental aspect in human existence, how the place one occupies constitutes one's being. This placial aspect of being, irreducible to mortality as well as to measured space, is what Heidegger seems to have become aware of in his later works. Casey, deeply indebted to Heidegger, refers to this later Heidegger's distinctions of "location" and "region" from space (p. xv). Heidegger also came to express a kind of nostalgia in lamenting the contemporary human situation that we are no longer grounded or rooted in a place we can call "home." This was related to the global spread of technology, which reduces the place of dwelling to calculability, thereby erasing or covering-over the unique or singular homeliness of a place with the homogeneity of measured space. This "homelessness" of the contemporary world is what Casey identifies as the very lack of a primal place, as being without the means of orientation in a complex and confusing world (p. xv). Casey takes over this Heideggerian critique of modernity, but extends the analysis of place into further depths. This importance of place in constituting our being and our understanding of being, has become an important philosophical topic over the last fifty years. Aside from Heidegger, many thinkers have written on the subject. The "phenomenological" study of place and what one might call an ontological spatiality, including the topics of alterity or otherness, distance, body, dwelling, etc.

have been developed within contemporary Continental thought in various directions by Buber, Bachelard, Sartre, Merleau-Ponty, Levinas, etc. On this side of the Atlantic most recently, Ed Casey has raised this issue of place to a primary concern in two books published during the nineties. While Casey expresses his indebtedness to Heidegger, a detailed development of the explicit distinction between place as a unique singularity and space as homogeneous and measurable, is a contribution we can ascribe to Casey in this work.

I tend to think that this recognition of the importance of place by many thinkers is indicative of our contemporary age. The making-explicit of place can be traced to the technological developments of modernity which enigmatically has also led to the obscuring-leveling of place. For example, the spread of technology has allowed for the increased speed and efficiency of both physical travel and information travel. Distances are abolished with the increase in speed, efficiency, and ease in travel and communication, bringing the far near and displacing human existence into alien lands. On one level, this has resulted in the globalization of consumer "culture" on a mass scale, to threaten with homogenization the unique ways of life of the indigenous cultures of the world. The brushing aside of the different, sweeping it under the rug of sameness made possible by mass consumerism, makes many of us long for the home-place from which we have been uprooted, the place which provided the secure ground of being. The easy access and high speed of travel and communication, made possible by the latest technology, has shrunk this globe to make obvious the multiplicity of cultural places, previously isolated or far from one another. The result seems to be that we are faced with the extreme contrast between the superficial homogeneity of consumer pseudo-culture and the rich multiplicity of differences amongst world cultures. Alongside the leveling homogenization, there also results the increasing pronouncement of differences between previously isolated ways of living, the explicit abundance and multiplicity of claims to the proper way of being. Given this diversity of places, each claiming autonomy and this very autonomy become threatened with erasure, the importance of place becomes explicit in its struggles against this erasure. This is one reason that thinkers like Casey cannot help but notice the importance of place in the constitution of our ways of being. In this speed-bound era of increased mobility, this threat of placelessness, according to

Casey, results in disorientation and dispossession, the experience of being unplaced (p. xii & xiv). This condition of an apparent placelessness is pronounced as we too easily rush from place to place, displaced without a home-place to return to. But resisting and struggling against this onslaught of globalized placelessness, there is what Casey considers to be the cultural dimension of place, dense with affiliated historical, social, and political aspects (p. 33). Although this is not necessarily a central focus of Casey's work, it seems to me that it is in the context of the globalization of technology and capitalism that the importance of place comes to be recognized by Heidegger and a Heidegger-influenced phenomenologist such as Casey.

Casey's contention is that the place one occupies has everything to do with what and who one is as well as that one is (p. xiii); that one's very being is place-oriented. In part one of *Getting Back into Place*, he points out the importance of place in both the navigation through and orientation to the world. Here he convincingly shows the independence of place from space, its distinction from the indifference of space-time, and questions the temporocentrist dogma that time is the first of all things (p. 14). He also discusses the significance of place in creation myths, mental nature, and rhetoric, and criticizes the modernist efforts to reduce place to space (p. xvi). Place is shown to be the ontological condition of existing things (p. 15), and even time cannot be without a place situating it (p. 21). Place as supporting and reflecting one's existence bounded by a double horizon of body and landscape, near and far (p. 29), as lived and thus also cultural or communal (p. 31), is distinguished from space (German *Raum*) as measurable and homogeneous (p. 22). Being cultural also means that place is historical (p. 31), in distinction from the equably flowing time (p. 22). Casey here is convincing in his argument that with the rise and spread of Western modernity, the uniformity of space and equability of time have displaced the priority of place, thus resulting in the current placelessness of our times, the feeling of nostalgia for a lost home or identity (p. 38).

In part two, he explores the role of the lived body in relating one to one's place, as well as the placial role played by dimension and directionality and thus orientation. Taking over from Aristotle, the body is shown to provide orientation to the dimensions of above and below, right and left, front and back, here and there (p. 45). Since without body, one would be disoriented, the living and moving body is shown as providing one with place (p. 48). There is also a detailed analysis of the various dimensions or meanings of "here" in its relation to "there," provided by the body (p. 52). Without the embodied orientation of here-there, there would be no place but rather a mere site (belonging to homogeneous space) (p. 65). Casey goes on to discuss the dimensions of here-there and near-far as linking body and world, providing a place for existence (p. 73), and discusses the spatial dimensions of right-left, above-below, front-back, as referring to the body's being-in-place (p. 76). Together these pairs are considered as the five dyads providing our bodily existence with worldly place.

Bodily orientation leads to the discussion in part three of the structures of dwelling, the role of architecture as built place, and how we dwell in such places. In this part, a lot of references are made to Heidegger who also worked in the fifties on the relation between building and dwelling. Buildings provide mediation between the skillful body and artless earth, between culture and nature (p. 112). The creation of such places not only transforms the landscape but also transforms our selves in constituting a mode of dwelling (p. 111) since buildings are an enlargement of our worldly embodiment (p. 120). But here as architect, the body is not only situated in place but is also actively situating (p. 116). In building places of dwelling, the self also hermeneutically constructs its own way of existing. Alongside the discussion of houses and cities, Casey here touches upon gardens and parks as cultivated places, with their capacity of exhibiting a various range of relations between the naturally given and the intentionally cultivated (p. 168). In any case place, as permitting our dwelling, is again shown to be ontologically prior to site and space.

As built places are surrounded, whether mediately or immediately, by the natural world, part four is dedicated to the discussion and investigation of places that are uncultivated and unbuilt, wild places as places that resist our human presence. It seems to make sense that the current thoughtful emergence of place from obscurity as a hidden ontological constituent of being also has special implications for our relation to and understanding of our natural environment. Globalization's violence towards the places of indigenous cultures is also extended towards nature, in its plundering of the environment without concern or respect for the place of nature or our place within nature. Environmental hazards have made it become increasingly questionable whether the attempt to colonize nature and rape its source of energy for the sole purpose of our consumption is proper in respect towards that which always exceeds our conceptual and technological grasp. That was the context within which I chose to read these sections in part four dedicated to wild places. This would be the part of this work most interesting to readers of this issue of *Vera Lex* focusing on the environment.

Casey in part four raises the necessity of questioning the marginalization of non-human nature at the periphery of the cultivated world, the anthropocentric assumption that nature is secondary to the human realm. He asks: What if nature is the true a priori and center? (p. 186). What is being questioned is the idealistic tendency of Western metaphysical thought. Rather than man or mind, nature may be prior as it is all encompassing and is that from which man and mind emerged. If that is the case we ought to respect nature in its own terms; and only this will allow us to recognize the deeper commonality of the human and the natural, according to Casey (p. 187). The discussion covers the experience of desolation one often undergoes when moving from domestic places to wild places, a movement explained as that from the familiarity of a customary place or center of residence, to the far-out uncentered or ec-centric insecurity of a new place (p. 195). Most interesting is how he ties together the above topics in his discussion of humanocentrism's threat of reappropriating nature and wilderness for human purposes. This happens for example even when the above-mentioned desolation is understood as a merely psychological matter concerning we human beings. But beyond human subjectivity, desolation points to nature in its resistance to human appropriation, the wilderness as not easily reduced to cultivated places. And it is in this sense that nature and wilderness, in their autonomy and autochthony, are sublime (p. 199). Nature and the wild is what constantly surrounds us, not only on land but as the sky (p. 207-8). Beyond its association with land and earth, one basic feature of wilderness, according to Casey, is ground (p. 212). The ground is what provides support, the basis-place or anchoring point for motion and experience, so that we can experience wild places, and gain orientation in and toward a wilderness area (p. 213). What I find significant in Casey's discussion here is that nature as sky is always above us, even when we are in the domesticated place of a big city; and nature as ground is always below us, providing a firm basis for experiencing our environment, even if that environment is one of built places. It is not only in the wilderness but also in the man-made world, that nature (*phusis*) is all-pervading and surrounds us. Only thus can we be oriented towards the non-human. This also means that we ought not to ignore this deep and often forgotten relationship of nature with our being. There is also an interesting discussion of the all-pervasiveness of nature as the atmosphere (p. 119). It is pointed out that the atmosphere is a large component of the "biosphere" of which all life-forms are a part (p. 221-2). This should be significant in understanding what, as life-forms, our relation to nature should be.

Casey goes on to discuss in detail the mutual relationship of nature and culture. The root meaning of culture and cultivation is traced to the Latin *colere*, to take care of, occupy, dwell; and this meaning is further related to the land and the soil one dwells in (p. 230-1). Casey interprets such etymological roots to indicate that the natural and the cultural are not as disparate as we often think them to be (p. 230). On the one hand, the wilderness is not culture-free as it is appropriated by and to culture in various ways (p. 234-5). But on the other hand, the wilderness is not necessarily culture-bound since the land or the sea in its wildness in many ways resists colonization efforts (p. 237). However, this does not mean that there is some absolute wilderness in-itself utterly impervious to cultural categories (p. 237-8). The natural and the cultural, each, in attempting to exclude its other, cannot help but incorporate its other into itself; and in this mutual invasion, the two alterities of nature and culture, must coexist (p. 239). At this point one might wonder what implications this mutuality of nature and culture would have to the above-mentioned a-priority of nature. Although he does not make an explicit clarification of this point, as he should, Casey does however make a strong case in showing how the fates of nature and culture have been intertangled ever since human beings emerged on the earth (p. 240). He exclaims that in a certain sense we are already at one with nature through a luminous wildness held in common (p. 246). In walking, building, and any creation of a work (for example in art), as Heidegger himself showed, the elements of earth ("nature") and of world ("culture") enter into struggle and commingle into a final commonality (p. 254). Everything is both natural and cultural not only in us, but also in the nature (p. 252). This means that since the thick density of the mutual embroilment of nature and culture is not human alone, it cannot be subsumed under the nomos ["law"] of human law or management. But neither can this be forced under the chthon ["earth", "ground"] of deep nature itself. Here culture and nature, autonomy and autochthony, conjoin in a common ground and law. Casey writes that the language, which is law (nomos), can be heard from the earth as well as articulating wildness within us and in nature alike (p. 256). The implications this may have for natural law theory, not explicated by Casey, is begging to be worked out.

In the context of our present situation, what is to be noted here is that the pre-established harmony between culture and nature has been destroyed, their equilibrium too easily disrupted, by the postindustrial contemporary landscape which has come to possess and reshape the wilderness. Most interestingly, Casey points out how this also explains why Americans turn to wilderness in whatever form it can be found or packaged, even under its obvious artificial form in Disney World or Safari Park (p. 258-9). This should remind us of our earlier mentioned point concerning the all-invasiveness of global capital, here constructing artificial places technologically supported, urging us to not question where the real wild places have gone. The escape from this artificiality and out into a richer and wider world, Casey believes, is through a reconnection with the earth. Every culture has its place in some natural environment. Rather than imposing ourselves on the earth, we need to let the land surrounding us be the guiding force; the solution is to be ecocentric rather than humanocentric (p. 260). This ecocentrism leads to lococentrism (p. 263). Casey seems to intimate that to be aware of our natural surroundings is to be aware of our place. The question of the place nature and its "law" holds for us within this 21st-century globalized world, and the place we occupy within nature as always exceeding our grasp, is now being felt as critical to our being at this turn of the millennium. This part of Casey's work exemplifies this feeling. Although Casey himself is not concerned with the theory of natural law, his work may provide some insight to those interested in this concept. The "law of nature"—whatever it be—certainly ought to be heard, and Casey's point may be intimated to mean that rather than being ego- and humanocentric, an ecocentric stance leading to lococentrism will allow us to hear this.

In the final part, Casey looks at the nature of journeys as the experience of being between places, and at the meaning of home-place, homecoming, and homesteading. Since place resists any confinement to precise spatial-temporal parameters, Casey sees place as providing the changing but indispensable material medium of journeys, as way stations as well as destinations and origins of these journeys (p. 274). In this part Casey alludes to the specific placial condition of contemporary times, in which disoriented individuals drift within the indifferent spaces of housing developments, shopping centers, and superhighways (p. 275). We might add that such indifferent spaces are becoming more evident around the globe, covering-over the cultural differences of unique places. From this modern nomadism of drifting through homogeneous space, Casey distinguishes the journey as being deeply engaged with the heterogeneity of places it encounters (p. 279). In discussing the topic of place as home, Casey mentions the connection between the spirit of a people and place as made evident in their regional character (dialects, gestural styles, ways of thinking) (p. 304). Persons who dwell in places come to share certain features with the local landscape while also making a mark upon that land (p. 305). So the relation here is reciprocal, person and place co-constitute one another's way of being. But this also means that what poses a threat to our implacement as reflected in our personal identity, threatens our sense of well-being, and may result in alienation from the place one previously felt a part of (p. 307). The erasing of a sense of belonging to a peculiar place brought upon in this contemporary world results not only in the sense of displacement but also the sense that one has nowhere to go (p. 309). This can be taken literally, such as in the case of indigenous tribes being displaced from one region to another by national governments; or the case of peoples being dispossessed of the land they occupied for generations, due to unending wars or invasions, and having to immigrate from one country to another that they feel reluctant to call "home". But what is significant is the "existential" fact that no longer does any single place seem to offer an abode for a fuller selfhood (p. 309); the self has no home amongst the indifferent sites or homogenous spaces offered by modern globalist pseudo-culture. Casey's point is that since to be is to be in place, with this loss of place, we lose touch with our own most being. What is needed, therefore, is a renewed appreciation of place, a conclusion I am in agreement with.

The postmodern phenomenon of displacement, Casey writes, has a lot to do with our contemporary failure to link up with places, places local as well as occupied by cities and regions, cultures and societies, and the natural world (p. xiv). While ignored by the modern thinkers, the contemporary feeling of a loss of place as replaced by mere sites has resulted in the distinctively postmodern wish to return to place (p. xiv). This nostalgia for a home-place is directed not only towards a culture claimed as one's own, but also towards nature. For we also become nostalgic over places now inaccessible and despoiled by ecological damage or negligence (p. 38). Casey takes this contemporary feeling of not being secured in place, of being seemingly out of place—the disorientation, displacement, and destabilization of post-modern times—to mean that we ought to explicitly reflect upon what it means to be in place. Casey admits that the anxiety of being without place would be justified in a placeless Newtonian or Cartesian desert, but then reminds us that this world is packed with places (p. 104). The suggestion is that the awareness of place as such would solve our homelessness. However, I think that it is also necessary to recognize as significant in this matter that the disparate places with which the postmodern world is packed are multiple and in flux, rapidly emerging and vanishing, coming and going. One might argue that the anxiety is that of having to continuously choose from amongst this shifting multiplicity of available options. Packed with too many places, each struggling against obscurity for recognition, beneath the surface of the oblivious totalitarianism of consumer pseudo-culture, postmodernity no longer assures us of any stability. The postmodern man is truly homeless and in a state of limbo. Casey's work here provides an important and necessary contribution to the current ongoing discussion concerning the pervasiveness of place in constituting human existence, whether of the self or of the collective. Although Casey does not explicitly focus upon the contemporary conditions of placelessness in its relations to global technology and capitalism, resulting in the rapid fluctuations of multiple places, this topic will surely be taken up by future thinkers of place, taking over from where Casey left off. One of the major impacts from reading this work is that perhaps we ought to loosen our will to grasp *a priori*, and instead learn to listen to what is other than ourselves—the autochthonous and autonomous voices of nature and of culture, thus recognizing our proper place. However, whether nostalgia is the only proper response in this situation ought to be questioned as well.

THE TRAVAIL OF NATURE: THE AMBIGUOUS ECOLOGICAL PROMISE OF CHRISTIAN THEOLOGY

By Paul H. Santmire. Minneapolis: Fortress, 1985

Review by Thomas D. O'Sullivan
Department of Philosophy and Religious Studies, Pace University

One of the most indispensable tools for the serious student of environmental values is an historical overview of the theology of nature in the Christian tradition, a survey that is comprehensive but concise, scholarly but readable. H. Paul Santmire's *The Travail of Nature* has for some years supplied that tool. Santmire provides a quick summary, analysis, comparison, and critique of the place of the natural environment in the theological thought of a series of major Christian thinkers, most notably of Irenaeus, Origen, Augustine, Aquinas, Bonaventure, Francis of Assisi, Luther, Calvin, Barth, and Teilhard de Chardin.

He carries out this project quite well, though his topic is so broad and each subdivision of it so complex that it can scarcely be expected that a well-informed reader will be perfectly satisfied with every one of his judgments. This is more a consequence of the scope of Santmire's book than of the quality of his scholarship. In my opinion, Santmire exaggerates the importance of Irenaeus, but it would be difficult to argue that he underestimates the value of Origen as a proponent of environmental values since Origen does show less esteem for embodied human life and therefore for material nature than perhaps any other so eminent Christian theologian. Surely Santmire's discussion of Bonaventure is more heavily in debt to two or three secondary publications—as opposed to Bonaventure's own writings—than seems appropriate even for a cursory survey of this sort. And he fails to do justice (but who could?) to the subtleties of Thomas Aquinas and Karl Barth.

There are two unfortunate and rather surprising gaps in Santmire's historical survey. The first is the absence of writers from the Byzantine tradition. After Origen, Santmire discusses the ideas of Western figures from Augustine down to the twentieth century. Clearly a book of this length cannot possibly deal with every Christian writer who has had something interesting to say about the natural environment, but I suspect that the Eastern tradition, in the writings of figures like Gregory of Nazianzus, Maximus the Confessor, John of Damascus, and Symeon the

New Theologian—perhaps even more in the exquisite theological poetry of an Ephrem the Syrian or a Romanos the Melodist—may well have some really important material to contribute to Santmire's discussion.

A second regrettable lacuna is represented by the absence of women's perspectives. For centuries, theology was looked upon as an almost exclusively masculine preserve, but in the last couple of generations the number of female theologians has increased, and the importance of the great women writers of the past such as Teresa of Avila has been reaffirmed. Most important, feminist theologians have plausibly suggested that the different experiences of women help prepare them to make a distinct and very valuable contribution to theological reflection. Ecofeminist writers in particular have drawn most interesting parallels between the consequences of androcentric attitudes toward women and those of anthropocentric attitudes toward nature. It is especially in the section dealing with medieval thought that Santmire's book seems distorted by the absence of women's voices. He makes no reference to Hildegard of Bingen, for example, who wrote so much about the world of nature.

When all is said and done, however, the historical survey is the most valuable part of this book, and readers are certainly in Santmire's debt for assembling so many disparate materials from different phases of the development of Christian thought, all of which discuss human beings' relationship with the natural environment from a theological point of view.

Unfortunately, Santmire imposes a complicated and idiosyncratic structure upon his materials which often threatens to become a distraction. He identifies what he calls three root metaphors: the metaphor of ascent, the metaphor of fecundity, and the metaphor of migration to a good land. He identifies also what he calls two theological motifs: the spiritual motif (deriving from the first root metaphor) and the ecological motif (deriving from the second and third). He systematically discusses the authors about whom he writes in terms of the relationship he discerns between their ideas and these motifs and metaphors. So we read jargon-burdened discussions, for example, about "the uncertain legacy of the subordination of the metaphor of fecundity to the metaphor of ascent at the roots of Thomas's hierarchical thinking …. the uncertain legacy of a theology which is virtually untouched by the metaphor of migration to a good land" (94).

Santmire's concepts are not without interest, and if his project in this book were to develop an original ecotheology they might well be appropriate. It is praiseworthy, perhaps, to want to probe the "intuitive as well as cognitive, subliminal as well as self-conscious, tacit as well as articulated" (14) sources that underlie theological reflection, but in my opinion these root metaphors and theological motifs contribute very little that is of value to Santmire's effort to elucidate the thought of figures such as Augustine, Aquinas, and Luther. Surely it is quite a large enough task to try to do justice to the self-conscious, articulated work that they actually produced.

Augustine, Aquinas, Luther, and all the other theologians with whom Santmire deals, were of course entirely unaware of these metaphors and motifs as influences upon their thinking. On the other hand, every one of them strongly acknowledged the authority of one document—I of course mean the Bible—and historical theology enables us to discover with considerable subtlety the varying hermeneutic postures that they took toward that document.

It seems to me that within the Bible there are two pairs of themes that are strongly relevant to the problem of our relationship to the natural environment. The first pair is the theme of the goodness of God's creation (Gen. 1:31) and the contrasting theme of the wide-ranging effects of human wickedness—most strikingly expressed in the line "cursed is the ground because of you" (Gen. 3:17). The second pair is the theme of human dominion over the fish, the birds, and the beasts (Gen. 1:28) and the contrasting or perhaps complementary theme of the solidarity of all living things—which is reflected directly or indirectly in episodes as various as the effort of God to provide Adam with a fit companion (Gen. 2:18-19) and the fasting of the animals along with the people of Nineveh (Jonah 3:7-8), but which is expressed most notably in the covenant which God makes after the universal deluge "with every living creature" (Gen. 9:10) and most picturesquely I suppose in the line "ask the beasts, and they will teach you" (Job 12:7).

The advantages of discussing the thought of an Augustine, an Aquinas, or a Luther in terms with which he was consciously familiar are obvious, but I would say that there is another reason for the usefulness of Biblical themes in the discussion of environmental theology. That is that it situates the discussion at the center of the history of Christian thought.

The first pair of themes that I spoke of in the last paragraph is fundamental to discussions about the "problem of evil," for example, while the second is central to Christian anthropology.

It is only after completing his survey of Christian literature from the patristic period to the twentieth century that Santmire turns his attention to the Bible and makes an attempt "to develop an ecological reading of biblical faith" (189). He considers the Hebrew Bible first, then the New Testament. He takes his starting point from the fact that most modern Bible scholars believe that "The Bible has to do primarily with history, not with nature" (176). He cites G. W. H. Lampe as an example of the kind of writer with whom he takes issue, saying that according to Lampe "God's revelation to Israel came primarily to Israel in terms of election, covenant, and the manifestation of judgment and salvation in the events of national history, not through the natural order" (184). He seeks to balance if not replace this reading with a reading that would emphasize what he calls a "theology of the land in the Old Testament" (190).

The problem with Santmire's proposal is that, in the Hebrew Bible, the land of Canaan is indeed seen as holy, in the final analysis, because of its place in the history of election and covenant rather than because of its place in nature. What I mean is that what is really important about the land that God promises to Abraham and delivers into the hands of his descendants is not its beauty or its fertility, but the fact that it is given by God to His people as part of the divine plan for their liberation. Contrary to what Santmire says, the historical value of the land is from a Biblical perspective incomparably greater than its natural value.

On the other hand, Santmire seems to me to be on firmer ground when he turns to the problem of reading the New Testament, and tries to discover an openness to what we would think of as an ecological perspective on nature in its inescapably soteriological and eschatological message. He delineates two alternate visions of God's final goal for the world: first "a glorified kingdom of spirits alone who, thus united with God, may contemplate him in perfect bliss, while as a precondition of their ecstasy all the other creatures of nature must be left by God to fall away into eternal oblivion" (217) and second "a glorious city of resurrected saints who dwell in justice, blessed with all the resplendent fullness of the earth, and who continually call upon all creatures to join with them in their joyful praise of the one who is all in all" (217-18).

Santmire may be correct in saying that the first view—which he would characterize as more "spiritual"—is the view of most Christian interpreters of the Bible today. It certainly seems to be the view of the majority of ordinary Christian lay people. But I think he overestimates its influence in the authentic theological tradition. Surely the second view, which avoids heterodox "spiritualizing" tendencies and sees eternal life in terms of the resurrection—what Santmire would consider the "ecological" view—is the traditional and the authoritative teaching of the Christian churches.

Santmire is not wrong (except stylistically) when he speaks of a "struggle between the spiritual and the ecological motifs" (182), but I suspect that the struggle is more in evidence on the level of popular religious culture than of theology. Perhaps, for the theologically-oriented reader, the most valuable aspect of the book is its depiction of the contrast between two Christian anthropologies: the orthodox view of human beings as by nature embodied and therefore in relation with the material universe, and the Gnostic/"New Age" view of embodiment as a source or at least a sign of evil to be minimized and superseded.

PLATO'S DEMOCRATIC ENTANGLEMENTS: ATHENIAN POLITICS AND THE PRACTICE OF PHILOSOPHY

By S. Sara Monoson. Princeton, NJ:
Princeton University Press, 2000

Reviewed by Harold Brown
Department of Philosophy and Religious Studies, Pace University

S. Sara Monoson has written a good book, although one which is interestingly flawed. However, since the book has so many fine qualities, its flaws do not seem to lessen our interest.

In a structural sort of way, the most serious flaw is the omission of a bibliography.[1] In her "Acknowledgements" Monoson does list the Platonic texts, translations and major commentaries she used. There is also a comprehensive Citation index, listing citations to classical literature, i.e., to the Greek poets, historians and orators as well as to Plato's dialogues. There is some compensation for the omission of a general bibliography by the fact that the general index lists names of authors cited in both text and in footnotes throughout the book. So, if one becomes interested in a particular text after it has been cited two, three or four times in a given chapter, rather than paging back to find the first, and only complete, citation in that chapter, one can look in the general index. At worst, with an author with multiple citations, one has then only to look at a relatively small number of pages. But having a bibliography—even just an alphabetical listing—would be a tremendous help.

What are some of the strengths of this book? First, in its frame of reference, this is a scholarly work of extraordinary breadth. The bibliographical listing put together by this reviewer, including references from fewer than half of the chapters of this relatively short book, includes almost 200 monographs, articles and book chapters (hence the interest in a general bibliography). In many cases, Monoson's references, mostly in footnotes but sometimes in the text, include very helpful information about the thesis, strengths, weaknesses, topics covered, or other important material about the book or article in question. In addition, the scholarly works to which she refers are from a range of disciplines, including polit-

[1]A curious omission, in light of the fact that this work began as a doctoral dissertation. Perhaps the omission of a general bibliography was an editorial decision.

ical philosophy and political theory, literary criticism, classics, history, philosophy and, undoubtedly, a few others.

Secondly, the book is well planned. Part One investigates various "aspects of Athenian democratic thought," using "... a growing literature in classics and political theory that considers Athenian political life fluidly to reach beyond the functioning of specific traditional political institutions" (9). In Part Two Monoson considers some of the dialogues, emphasizing that "... a new reading of Plato's treatment of democracy becomes possible only once features of the Athenian civic self-image are juxtaposed with Plato's account of philosophical practice." This reading is in turn based on five different elements of recent Plato scholarship:

> First, work tracing the roots of the new genre of writing Plato develops, philosophic dialogue, in Athenian drama (specifically tragedy). . . .
> Second, the compelling body of literature on why Plato wrote dialogues. . . .
> Third, the few historical studies of Plato...fourth...are the several efforts to consider the complexities of the relationship between Socrates and Athenian democracy. . .fifth. . .is the work. . .reassessing Plato's treatment of democracy (9-12)

More specifically, Part One looks at "...aspects of the Athenian self-image." These chapters "...show that orthodox Athenian democratic thought strongly identified the achievement of democracy with the accomplishment of social unity, an intellectually capable citizenry, the responsible exercise of power, relations of reciprocity among citizens and between city and individual, and the defeat of tyranny"(16). To achieve her goal, Monoson examines various accounts of the story of Harmodius and Aristogeiton,[2] the idea of the citizen as a "frank speaker (*parrhesiastes*), the citizen as lover (*erastes*), with particular reference to the use of this metaphor in Pericles' Funeral Oration[3] and the metaphor of the citizen as theater goer (*theates*).

Part Two then builds on Part One. As a result of the context developed in Part One, there are now "new questions about the relationship of

[2]The classical sources for this story include Herodotus, *History*, 5.69-72 and 6.123; Thucydides, *The Peloponnesian War*, 1.20.2, 6.54.1-1-59.4; Plato, *Hipparchus;* Aristotle, *The Constitution of Athens*, 18.1-19.2

[3]Thucydides, 2.34-46.

his thought to the practice of democracy at Athens" (17). In Chapter Five Monoson reviews six factors that have in the past been used to demonstrate Plato's hostility to democracy:

1. Plato's own aristocratic heritage;
2. Plato's reaction to Socrates' last years, namely, the attempt by the Thirty to involve him in their operations and then his condemnation after the restoration of the democracy;[4]
3. Plato's low esteem for the "common man" and consequent antagonism to majority rule;
4. The "founding" in *Republic* of an autocratic regime;
5. The founding of the Academy in Athens;
6. Plato's involvement in Syracusan politics.[5]

Chapters Six, Seven and Eight attempt to connect the practice of philosophy with three prevalent modes of Athenian civic discourse: frank speaking; the funeral oration; and theorizing. In Chapter Six, Monoson demonstrates the relationship between the philosopher and the frank speaker in *Laches, Gorgias, Republic* and *Laws*. In Chapter Seven, she uses the funeral oration in *Menexenus* to explicate first Plato's critique of Pericles and, second, "the links between philosophic practice and ... public funeral oratory." Finally, in Chapter Eight she shows how Plato "models his depiction of philosophic practice on ... the intellectual labors of the ordinary theater-going public" (17).

By and large, she accomplishes what she sets out to do—with considerable success. The four chapters in Part One are quite well written; Monoson knows her sources and uses them extremely well.

To describe some of the issues I have with the book, we need to look more closely at what Monoson tells us she plans to accomplish in her book. In the first paragraph of her Introduction, entitled "Siting Plato," she writes, "In this book I argue for a fundamental rethinking of the relationship between Plato's thought and the practice of democracy." One

[4]On Socrates and the Thirty Oligarchs, see Plato's *The Apology of Socrates*, 32C-E, as well as Plato's *Seventh Letter*, 324D-324C. On his trial and condemnation, in addition to Plato's account of his defense speech, see *The Apology of Socrates*, see Plato's *Seventh Letter*, 325B-D.

[5]The best classical source for Plato's activities in Syracuse are his *Seventh and Eighth Letters*.

very important reason for constructing this argument is "that the canonical view of Plato as a virulent antidemocrat is not sound." According to Monoson, what is really happening in Plato's work is that:

> a searching consideration of the possibilities raised by some democratic ideals and institutions coexists alongside severe criticisms of democratic life and politics. Plato finds the lived experience and ideology of Athenian democracy repulsive and fascinating, troubling and intriguing. He not only assails democratic practice but also weaves hesitations about the reach of that attack into the very presentation of his thought. A substantial measure of ambivalence, not unequivocal hostility, marks his attitude toward democracy as he knew it. (p. 3)

Several issues have to be raised in connection with this first paragraph. The first point is that Monoson unquestionably provides sufficient documentation to show that Plato is not a "virulent antidemocrat," that is, assuming it is possible to actually know Plato's personal political leanings.[6] Second, and related to the first point, I am concerned when someone tells me that he or she is going to explain to me something about Plato's thought.[7] Third, and continuing in the same direction as the first two points, I am not at all sure how a contemporary author could know that Plato found "...the lived experience and ideology of Athenian democracy *repulsive* [my emphasis]...." It really does seem to be somewhat important to draw a distinction between the wide variety of philosophical arguments that can be derived from the dialogues and Plato's thoughts about those arguments or about anything else. This distinction is crucially necessary precisely because of the nature of those dialogues. That Monoson is aware of the importance of the dialogue form is made abundantly clear by the second of the five strands of Plato scholarship: "the compelling body of literature on why Plato wrote dialogues." She goes on to write: "This work demonstrates that the dialogic form has deep

[6]From the Seventh Letter it appears that Plato was uniformly opposed to all forms of existing regimes. But in that letter, as in all of Plato's writing, his "agenda"—frequently in some sense educational—makes it difficult to take everything he writes absolutely at face value.

[7]See also the reference above to p. 17: "new questions about the relationship of his thought."

philosophic import. It is not simply a clever way to express a doctrine that could have been more easily stated in systematic exposition" (10). So then why is the dialogue form so important? What, for Monoson is the significance of the "compelling body of literature on why Plato wrote dialogues?" Monoson explains that this literature "supports my view that defining aspects of Plato's thought have roots in Athenian practice." The dialogue is "a mode of writing that allows Plato to craft for the reader the unusual experience of philosophic inquiry and dramatize both its departures from and attachments to Athenian traditions"[8] (10).

This leads us to more serious considerations: Monoson's use of both critical as well as classical literature; her strategy for "reading" Plato; and her understanding of the relationship between Plato's thought and the "practice of philosophy." With respect to the first of these concerns: the danger inevitably involved with the enunciation of a program such as Monoson's is that the reader begins to wonder about her selection and use of examples. For example, in Chapter Two she brings to light an impressive number of sources to explicate the relationship of the Athenian "practice of democracy with that of free speech" (51). In Chapter six she claims that Plato "defends the specifically democratic conceptualization of parrhesia and appropriates it for philosophy." Specifically, "he appropriates it to depict the difficult relationship between philosophic and democratic practice" (154).

Monoson presents a compelling argument for her position. Her argument shows that "Plato appropriates the ideal of parrhesia for philosophy." Moreover,

> Plato subtly manipulates its patriotic, political associations to illuminate the relation of this democratic practice to philosophy, as well as to engage his readers in thinking about how far a devotion to this democratic ideal will lead one, gently, to interest in philosophy. In Plato's usage parrhesia is an intellectually and morally significant ideal. (161)

But can we use Monoson's account, e.g., of parrhesia, to help us to understand the practice of philosophy, more generally, in the Platonic dia-

[8]In fact, all five of the strands of scholarship included for review and inclusion are used by Monoson either directly or indirectly to assist in her "effort to unsettle the common view that Plato's thought is at war with the Athenian democratic tradition" (9).

logues? Monoson's index of citations is extensive; but much is revealed by the dialogues she does not cite, e.g., *Euthyphro, Meno, Sophist, and Philebus*. Perhaps the most revealing is the absence of any reference to the *Meno*. Socrates tells Meno that a crucial difference between dialectics and eristics is that whereas in the verbal contest the Greeks called eristics the opponents are each trying to win a victory, in dialectics, the conversational partners are trying to reach the truth. As a result, the partners in dialectic should begin by coming to agreements about the meanings of important terms (75c-76a). Later in *Meno*, when he questions Meno's slave about the famous problem of the length of the side of the double square, Socrates emphasizes this point by the questions he poses to the slave, e.g., "Isn't this kind of figure called a square?" and "Doesn't a square have these four sides equal?" (82b). The questions Socrates asks the slave, with the commentary he offers to Meno, suggest that philosophy, at least as practiced by Socrates in certain circumstances, involves asking questions that are accessible to his interlocutor.

Ultimately, Monoson rests a great deal of her argument on the use of a relatively limited set of words and phrases, for example, parrhesiastes and parrhesia, eros and erastes, theates and theoros. The use of these terms in Plato's dialogues can be interpreted, as Monoson does interpret their use, to explicate the relationship between democratic thought and Plato's thought. However, as used comfortably and familiarly in the Socratic dialectic in any given context, when the conversation moves in a particular direction, that move might reveal as much about the nature of the interlocutor as it can about the topic in question—or in particular—about Plato's thought.

Monoson argues that the use of certain "democratic" terms explains the practice of Platonic philosophy. But one can persuasively argue that an understanding of the practice of Platonic philosophy explains the use not only of those "democratic" terms, but all others used in Plato's dialogues.

This leads to the third consideration. I referred above to the opening statement of Monoson' Introduction: "I argue for a fundamental rethinking of the relationship between Plato's thought and the practice of democracy." Earlier in her "Acknowledgements" Monoson writes: "I offer an interpretation of Plato that aims to expose his forging of a serious, though limited, alliance between the *practice of philosophy* and *Athenian demo-*

cratic politics [my italics]" (ix). The two claims suggest a close relationship between "the practice of philosophy" and "Plato's thought." Judging by the contents of her book, Monoson believes that "the practice of philosophy" refers to philosophy as practiced in Plato's dialogues (as perhaps practiced by Plato, privately). However, concerns about the possibility of grasping "Plato's thought" aside, the *Seventh Letter*, which Monoson cites about a dozen times, indicates some of the problems involved in trying to identify Plato's thought with anything he wrote.

Apart from the question of the legitimacy of trying to grasp "Plato's thought," Monoson does present some very strong arguments for the claim that Athenian democratic politics are inextricably woven into the fabric of Plato's dialogues and in that vein adds to Platonic scholarship an understanding of that "serious, though limited, alliance between the practice of philosophy and Athenian democratic politics."

Annotated Bibliography

Works especially illustrative of the focus of this issue—natural law and the environment—are emphasized below

ALEXANDER, Donald, "Bioregionalism: Science or Sensibility," *Environmental Ethics* 12 (1990): 161-173.

["A criticism of the bioregional movement in environmental philosophy for its unclear and incorrect philosophical and scientific concepts: e.g., definition of bioregion, boundaries of bioregion, and reverence for natural law. Bioregionalism should not be a scientific concept but a cultural sensibility, a social value. Region is a dialectical concept integrating both human and natural parameters."] From *International Society of Environmental Ethics Bibliography*. (Hereafter *ISEE*.)

ARNHART, Larry, "The Search for a Darwinian Science of Ethics," DIALOGOS: *An Interactive Journey of Science, Philosophy, and Theology*, issue 13. (See the review of Arnhart's *Darwinian Natural Right: The Biological Ethics of Human Nature*, in this issue.)

BENNETT, Jane and CHALOUPKA, William, eds. *In the Nature of Things: Language, Politics, and the Environment*. Minneapolis: University of Minnesota Press, 1993.

[Recent literary criticism and social theory are applied to the concept of "nature," which does not exist, according to the authors, independently of culture, particularly language. The contributors apply modern and post-modern theoretical approaches to such cultural items the Bible, science fiction, hunting, and green consumerism. A wide-ranging complement to ecofeminist critiques.] From *International Society for Environmental Ethics Newsletter*, summer, 1994, Vol. 5, no. 2: p.22.

BLUMM, Michael C. "The End of Environment Law? Libertarian Property, Natural Law, and the Just Compensation Clause in the Federal Circuit." *Environmental Law* 25 (no. 1, 1995): 171(p).

["Florida Rock Industries and Loveladies Harbor, two recent cases from the Federal Circuit, represent a radical, libertarian view of property and are not supported by either Supreme Court opinions or the history of American property law."] *Journal of Environmental Ethics* (Vol. 6, no. 1).

DES JARDINS, Joseph R. *Environmental Ethics: An Introduction to Environmental Philosophy*, Belmont, Calif.: Wadsworth Publishing Co., 1993 (2nd edition, 1997; the 3rd edition will be available in the winter of 2000). [Des Jardins' text is the first effort to write a history of philosophical environmental ethics over the last quarter century…There are, to be sure, now nearly a dozen attempts to write a systematic environmental ethics, but these books…do not attempt to survey the field of competing positions so much as to establish the author's own position as the most plausible one. Des Jardins tries to explain to beginners what has been going on in the field, and, given that goal, he does an excellent job.

Des Jardins' basic format is to combine a historical with a systematic introduction. Historically, he finds three periods: (1) an early model of "applied ethics," followed immediately by (2) "moral extensionism," and finally, on the contemporary scene, (3) "more radical environmental and ecological philosophies" (pp. viii-ix in the 1st edition, pp. x-xi in the 2nd edition).

Although the picture of a threefold historical development that parallels a systemic logical development of the field is only a rough guide, there is some truth in it; however, as is often the case, the history of ideas is messy. There are many strands, interwoven, interacting, or at times more or less independent. Des Jardins' format does enable him successfully to introduce most of these strands, even if they prove sometimes unruly.] From a review by Holmes Rolston III, *Environmental Ethics*, vol. 16, summer 1994.

FOSTER, John (Editor), *Valuing Nature? Economics, Ethics, and Environment*, London and New York: Routledge, 1997. 273 pp.

[Contemporary environmental economics has promoted the use of cost-benefit analysis in the design and choice of environmental policies. Cost-benefit calculations have in turn necessitated methods for monetary valuation of the environment, because the markets do not readily price many environmental goods and bads. Valuation methods typically use surrogate markets or hypothetical markets simulated in contingent valuation surveys to elicit monetary values for environmental goods or bads. The volume edited by John Foster criticizes this kind of monetary valuation and the use of its results in cost-benefit analyses, and outlines alternatives to them. The volume consists of fourteen articles written by economists, other social scientists, and philosophers.] From *Review of Social Economy*, fall 1998, Vol. 56, no. 3 p389 (5) by Jouni Paavola.

FRANCIONE, Gary L., *Animals, Property and the Law*. Philadelphia: Temple University Press, 1995.

[Current legal standards of animal welfare do not and cannot establish rights for animals. As long as they are viewed as property, animals will be subject to suffering for the social and economic benefit of human beings. The history of the treatment of animals, anticruelty statutes, vivisection, the Federal Animal Welfare Act, and specific cases such as the controversial injury of unanaestheized baboons at the University of Pennsylvania (Francione represented some 100 sit-in protestors at the National Institutes of Health, Bethesda, Maryland, over this issue). Francione argues that there is a paradoxical gap between our professed concern with the humane treatment of animals and the overriding practice of abuse permitted by U.S. law. Francione is professor of law at Rutgers University.] From *International Society for Environmental Ethics Newsletter*, summer 1995, Vol. 6, no.2, p.16.

FREYFOGLE, Eric T., "The Ethical Strands of Environmental Law," *University of Illinois Law Review*, 4, 1994.

[The morality that underlies the environmental movement, and the extent to which environmental statutes reflect this new moral order in environmental law. The U.S. Congress' acts and pronouncements do not form a coherent moral order, nor do they convey a vision of ecological wellbeing. In result, environmental lawmaking is approaching a crisis of vision and imagination, stumbling on knotty issues such as nonpoint-source water pollution and declining wildlife habitat. Principles that could guide environmental lawmaking oriented by encompassing more deep-rooted issues of ecosystem health. Freyfogle teaches law at the University of Illinois.] From *International Society for Environmental Ethics Newsletter*, summer 1995 v6, no.2, p.16.

FRIEND, Anthony M., "Economics, Ecology and Sustainable Development: Are They Compatible?" *Environmental Values*, vol. 2, no. 2 (1992): 157-170.

["The prevailing economic paradigm, in which a closed circular flow of production and consumption can be described in terms of 'natural laws' of the equilibrium of market forces, is being challenged by our growing knowledge of complex systems, particularly ecosystems. It is increasingly apparent that neo-classical economics does not reflect social, economic and environmental realities in a world of limited resources. The best way to understand the problems implicit in the concept of 'sustainable development' is provided by Ecological Economics—a new synthesis in which the traditional virtue of thrift is justified using modern ideas from systems theory and thermodynamics."] From *ISEE Bibliography*.

GARRETT, Jan, "Aristotle, Ecology, and Politics: Theoria and Praxis for the Twenty-First Century." In Creighton and Yeager Hudson, Eds, *Communication, Liberalism, and Social Responsibility* (Lewiston, NY: The Edwin Mellen Press, 1991). ["Studies in social and political theory, Vol. 14. Social philosophy today; no. 6 (papers from the International Social Philosophy Conference in Vermont in 1990). Environmental Philosophers frequently differ over whether the proper motivation for environmental concern is love of nature or concern for human good. Aristotelian conceptions of knowing, education, action, and community can be used to construct an attractive middle road. Although a certain kind of ecological knowledge disposes us to wish well toward the ecosystems with which our lives are entwined, this falls short of an adequate politics, which must make human beings the primary focus and appeal to the human good. Though ecosystems are communities that warrant appropriate respect, they cannot inspire as intense a commitment as can social communities. Anthropocentric arguments for preserving such ecosystems will have greater ethical force, because our duties to other humans are stronger and the sense of solidarity within human communities is greater."] (*International Society for Enviromental Ethics Newsletter* Vol. 5, no. 1).

George Wright Forum, vol. 10, no. 4, 1993, is a special issue on "Sustainability, Respect, and Responsibility," with thirteen articles. Examples: Edwin P. Pister, "Some Thoughts on Sustainability"; J. Baird Callicott, "Sustainability in a Historical-Philosophical Perspective"; Gary K. Meffe, "Sustainability, Natural Law, and the 'Real World'"; John J. Reynolds, "Sustainable Design and the U.S. National Park Service." Joseph C. Dunstan, Katherine L. Jope and Geoffrey M. Swan are guest editors. The George Wright Society is a nonprofit society for protected area professionals. The George Wright Society, P. O. Box 65, Hancock, MI 49930. From *ISSE Bibliography*.

HOSLE, Vittorio, "Philosophie der okologischen Krise, (Philosophy of the Ecological Crisis.) Munchen: Moskauer Vortrage. Beck'sche Reihe. 1991. [" I. Ecology as a new paradigm for politics. II. The Historical Roots of the Ecological Crisis. III. Ethical Consequences of the Ecological Crisis. IV. Economics and Ecology. V. Political consequences of the Ecological Crisis. Like Hans Jonas, to whom Hosle dedicates his book, Hosle believes that a fundamental shift in values is called for, a shift toward recognizing the absolute, non-relational value of nature. This consists in nature's teleology. At the same time, human teleology is, on account of its subjectivity, morally superior to the more simple forms of teleology found in the rest of nature. First presented at the Institute for Philosophy of the USSR Academy of Science in Moscow in 1990. Born in Milan in 1960, Hosle holds a full professorship in Essen, and is one of the youngest such philosophers in Germany."] (*International Society for Environmental Ethics Newsletter* Vol. 5. No. 1

MITTELSTRASS, J., "Umwelt und Gesundheit: Von der Schwierigkeit, sich mit Umwelt-und Gesundheitsstandards in einer Kulture-Natur zurechtzufinden [Ethics of Environment and Health: On the Environmental and Health Standards in a Cultural Nature]," in *Wiener Klinische Wochenschrift* 101, no. 17, 1989: 563-571.

[Scientific cultures, i.e. modern industrial societies, create their own environment. The expression denoting such a creation is a Kulture-Natur (cultural nature) determined by environmental and health standards. These standards are neither natural law nor can they be derived from nature. They are instead a part of human rationality. They also have an ethical dimension. The argument focuses on the following aspects: scientific and technological rationality as problem solver and problem producer, exploration of the concept of the Kulture-Natur, the status of environmental and health standards, presenting the case for the concept of rational ethics (Vernuftethik) against the concept of ecological ethics and the supplementation of a research imperative by an ethical imperative.]

NORTHCOTT, Michael S., *The Environment and Christian Ethics*. Cambridge: Cambridge University Press, 1996. 379 pp.

[" Of the books on environmental ethics written from a perspective of Christian ethics, Northcott's survey best knows the philosophical literature, in addition to having a thorough familiarity with the theological literature. Northcott sums up his argument: "The resolution of the environmental crisis requires the rediscovery of the existence of value and moral significance in the objective world prior to human acts of valuing, an independence which Western theists have traditionally located in the original act of divine beneficence in the creation of the world. . . . Without a recovery of this traditional recognition of the moral order and purposiveness of the world, prior to its processing by human perception, I do not believe it will be possible for modern societies ultimately to reduce their impacts on the ecological integrity of the nonhuman world" (pp. 92-93). In this search, Northcott is especially interested in philosophical arguments for intrinsic value in nature, which are congenial with this divine creation of value. Northcott recognizes amply that Christians have sometimes been the cause of environmental degradation; but he also believes that the primal Hebrew vision was "earth friendly" (p. 198), and that early Christianity with its understandings of the redemption of creation was also. The Christ is the Lord of nature, as well as of persons. Northcott argues for what he call a "repristination" of such worldviews (p. xiii, p. 239, p. 255). He has a soft spot for indigenous peoples, of whom he paints a rather rosy picture, and thinks that they were closer to the Hebrew mind than often realized. A central emphasis is on natural law, which Northcott hopes to recover."] (*Environmental Ethics*, Vol. 8, no. 3)

O'NEILL, John, *Ecology, Policy and Politics; Human Well Being and the Natural World*. London: Routledge, 1993. ["A Broadly Aristotelian account of welfare that reveals the relation between the good of non-humans and future generations and our own well-being. Welfare and liberal justifications of market based approaches to environmental policy fail, and this has implications for debates about market, civil society, and politics. Chapter titles: Nature, Justifying Cost-Benefit Analysis: Arguments from Welfare; Pluralism, Liberalism, and the Good life; Pluralism, Incommensurability, Judgement; Authority, Democracy and the Environment; Science, Policy and Environmental Value; Market, Household and Politics. Andrew Brennan, in the series, Environmental Philosophies, edits this book. O'Neill is lecturer in philosophy at

Lancaster University, Lancaster, UK. (*International Society for Environmental Ethics Newsletter* Vol. 5 no.1)

OTT, Konrad, *Okologie and Ethik: Ein Veruch praktischer Philosophie* (*Ecology and Ethics: An Attempt at Practical Philosophy.* Tubigen: Attempto Verlag, 1993.

[Otto's book has three main parts: 1. The Concept of Ecology. 2. Critical Theory and Nature. 3. Ecoethical Arguments. In part one, he discusses the history of the discipline of philosophy and various ecological approaches to environmental philosophy, such as human ecology, speculative ecology, including Schorsch's mystical holism, Roszak's subversive ecology, Hosle's objective idealism, and Christian ecology. In part two, he finds that we can learn from Adorno's and Horkheimer's views on nature, the early Habermas' view in his *Knowledge and Human Interests*, and the later Habermas' view in his ethical discourse writings. Part three presents a taxonomy of ecoethical arguments: a) utilitarianism, b) aestheticism, c) the human right to nature, d) ethics of compassion and ecological pathognomics, e) objective and subjective theories of value in nature, and f) evolutionism. Ott is widely read and draws on both German and English sources. He himself opts for a teleologically grounded physiocentric position, which he calls "ecological pathognomics" (p.144, pp153-155). He believes that we should further the good of telelogical nature for its own sake. Ott did his dissertation with Habermas in Frankfurt and is about to finish his habilitation (teaching qualification) in Tubingen. (Thanks to Angelika Krebs, University of Frankfurt.)] From *International Society for Environmental Ethics Newsletter*, summer 1994, Vol.5, no.2, p.26.

PANNENBERG, Wolfhart, *Toward a Theology of Nature: Essays on Science and Faith* edited by Ted Peters. (Philadelphia: Westminster/John Knox Press, 1993) p. 208.

["Many scholars of religion sit timidly by waiting to hear what physicists and biologists say about the world of nature. Then, they adjust their religious vision accordingly; but not systematic theologian Wolfhart Pannenberg. Based on dialogue between theologians and scientists for more than three decades, Pannenberg poses theological questions to natural scientists . . . He says the scientific view of nature is incomplete and challenges scientists to incorporate the idea of God into their picture of nature. He reviews the relationship between natural law and contingency, the importance of the spirit in the phenomenon of life, field theory language, and the theological account for the nature of God and of God's creative activity. Pannenberg believes the world we live in is a creature of a creating God, and unless we understand this, we cannot fully understand the world."] From *ISEE Bibliography.*

RACHELS, James, *Created From Animals: The Moral Implications of Darwinism.* (NY: Oxford University Press, 1990)

ROLSTON, Holmes, III. "Can and Ought We to Follow Nature?" *Environmental Ethics* 1 (1979): 7-30.

["Nature knows best" is reconsidered from an ecological perspective, which suggests that we follow nature. The phrase "follow nature" has many meanings. In an absolute law-of-nature sense, persons invariably and necessarily act in accordance with natural laws, and thus cannot but follow nature. In an artifactual sense, all deliberate human conduct is viewed as unnatural, and thus it is impossible to follow nature. As a result, the answer to the question, whether we can and ought to follow nature, must be sought in a relative sense according to which human conduct is sometimes more and sometimes less natural. Four specific relative senses are examined: a homeostatic sense, an imitative ethical sense, an axiological sense, and a tutorial sense. Nature can be followed in a homeostatic sense in which human conduct utilizes natural laws for our well-being in a stable environment, but this following is nonmoral since the moral elements can be separated from it. Nature cannot be followed in an imitative ethical sense because nature itself is either amoral or, by some accounts, immoral. Guidance for inter-human ethical conduct, therefore, must be sought not in nature, but in human culture. Nevertheless, in an axiological sense, persons can and ought to follow nature by viewing it as an object of orienting interest and value. In this connection, three environments are distinguished for human well-being in which we can and ought to participate—the urban, the rural, and the wild. Finally, in a tutorial sense, persons can and ought to follow nature by letting it teach us something of our human role, our place, and our appropriate character in the natural system as a whole. In this last sense, "following nature" is commended to anyone who seeks in his or her human conduct to maintain a good fit with the natural environment—a sense of following nature involving both efficiency and wisdom."]

SCHREINER, Susan E., *The Theater of His Glory: Nature and the Natural Order in the Thought of John Calvin.* (Durham, NC: Labyrinth Press, 1991) 164 pages.

["The concept of God's providence is a kind of arch that frames both the concept of nature and of grace in Calvin's thought. With sympathetic attention to Calvin's concept of natural law."] (*Environmental Ethics*, Vol. 3, no. 4)

SINGH, Rana P .B., ed., *The Spirit and Power of Place: Human Environnment and Sacrality*, Varanasi, India; National Geographic Society of India, 1994. ["Simultaneously published as the National Geographic Journal of India, vol. 40, 1994. Over two dozen articles. Examples: J. Donald Hughes, 'The Integrity of Nature and Respect for Place'; Amos Rapapport, 'A Critical Look at the Concept of Place', O. F. G. Stilwell, 'Sacred Space Reconsidered': Amita Sinha, 'Pilgrimage—Journey to the Sacred Landscape of Braj'; Alec Paul and Paul Simpson-Housley, 'The Manitoba Landscape of Martha Ostenso's *Wild Geese.*' And many others. Inquries to Dr. Rana P. B. Singh, Excutive Editor, NGJI, No.b29/12 A Lanka Varanasi, UP 221005, India] (*International Society for Environmental Ethics Newsletter* Vol. 5, number 2)

THOMPSON, Paul B. "Conceptions of Property and the Biotechnology Debate." *BioScience* 45 (no. 4, April 1995): 275-282.

["Philosophical concepts of property applied to biotechnology can help evaluate the relative strengths and weaknesses of arguments offered to justify alternative political positions. Two broad philosophical approaches to property are: (1) one in terms of rules to produce ethical goals such as social welfare or personal liberty, and (2) one that treats the property status of an entity as an ontological question. Natural law and labor theories are ontological approaches, the former influential in Europe. Protection through patents and copyrights has largely been defended on instrumental grounds, such as enhancing economic growth, especially in the United States."] (*Environmental Ethics*, Vol. 6, no. 1)

TRAINA, Cristina, "Baird Callicott's Ethical Vision: Response to Baird Callicott," *American Journal of Theology & Philosophy*, Vol. 18, no. 1 (January 1997): 81-87.

[The author finds Callicott's global ethic especially as articulated in J. Baird Callicott, *Earth Insights: A Multicultural Survey of Ecological Ethics from the Mediterranean Basin to the Australian Outback* (Berkeley: University of California Press, 1994) to "bear an uncanny resemblance to Roman Catholic natural law thinking." The points of resemblance include: the existence of universal ethical criteria; a vision of the common good (although Callicott's is larger in scope—global—and discussed within an ecological model); proper ethical behavior, fitting one's actions to the common good is, in some sense, "natural"; stewardship. The author next examines potential pitfalls associated with natural law theory to see if they apply equally to Callicott's position. Firstly, a genuine global ethic must speak to the experiences of all peoples, the oppressed as well as the privileged. Second, traditional natural law theory defines the person as a system with permanent ends with right action coordinated to those ends, whereas the more contemporary view of the person accounts for integration into historical circumstances, which justify change of function, at least slightly. Here Callicott's position proves superior to traditional natural law, but only slightly. Finally, how do individual human rights relate to the common good especially a common good augmented to include species and ecosystems?

Overall, the author views Callicott's global ethic as remedial for traditional natural law because its "postmodern perspective may actually help to seal some of the pitfalls mentioned above; for example, a worldview that expects continuing paradigm shifts is less likely to baptize a single view of relationships or one set of principles" (p. 85).

WILLIS, David J., "Ecophilosophy and Natural Law," *Journal of Energy, Natural Resources and Environmental Law* (University of Utah College of Law) 12 (no. 2, 1996): 419-451

["More effort is needed to construct and articulate a coherent ecophilosophy. . . . It is particularly vital that attention be focused on the philosophical underpinnings of environmental policy. . . .In a philosophical vacuum, we may do little to protect and preserve our conception of the good life" (p. 419, p. 422). "What we think about and wish for in environmental matters—what we value, both for ourselves and posterity—is the proper business of ecophilosophy and a timely subject for public debate. Natural law is a key element of this approach. . . . Ecophilosophy offers such a theory based upon the Gaia hypothesis, a concept of the earth as a unified biological/geological entity greater than the sum of its parts" (p. 423, p. 424). Willis offers ten principles of natural law, among them: "1. The commonwealth of nature constitutes the greater society of which all living beings are members and have a rightful place" (p. 429). "3. All forms of life have intrinsic as well as utilitarian value, adding to the diversity, health, and richness of the natural commonwealth" (p. 433). "10. Enlightened self-awareness and action on the part of individuals acts cumulatively to encourage the maturing of human society and bring it into better harmony with the natural order" (p. 449)."] (*Environmental Ethics*, Vol. 9, no. 4)

The Editor

CONTRIBUTORS

Alejandra Carrasco is Scholar in Residence at Catholic University of America, 2000 S Eads Street, Arlington, VA 22202

Peter P. Cvek is Associate Professor of Philosophy at Saint Peter's College, 2641 Kennedy Blvd., Jersey City, New Jersey 07306. Prof. Cvek is currently Director of Honors at St. Peter's. His research interests include history of ethics, especially natural law tradition, medical ethics and Asian philosophy.

Frank W. Derringh is Associate Professor of Philosophy at New York City Technical College of CUNY, 300 Jay Street, Brooklyn, NY 11201. Prof. Derringh teaches undergraduate courses in philosophy; his current interests are environmental philosophy and green political theory. He holds a Ph.D. in philosophy from Columbia University.

Guido Leidig is Member of the Board of the European Faculty of Land Use and Development, Leiter Abteilung Betriebswirtschaft, Bundesverband Druck und Medien e. V. Biebricher Allee 79, 65187 Wiesbaden. Dr. Leidig is a past contributor to *VERA LEX* and writes extensively on environmental issues.

Thomas B. Spademan is Assistant Professor of Philosophy at the University of Arkansas at Little Rock, 2801 S. University, Little Rock, AR 72204. Prof. Spademan received his Ph.D. in Philosophy from Purdue and a J. D. from University of Wisconsin Law School. He teaches business ethics in the executive MBA program and professional ethics in the Information Technology Program at UALR.

THE INTERNATIONAL NATURAL LAW SOCIETY ELECTS A NEW PRESIDENT

On June 14th the executive committee of the International Natural Law Society met on the Fordham University campus and elected Fr. Joseph W. Koterski, S. J. as the new president of the Society to succeed Professor Virginia Black. Fr. Koterski, a native of Cleveland, Ohio, received his A.B. in 1976 from Xavier University in Cincinnati with a major in classical languages. His M.A. and Ph.D. come from St. Louis University, where he wrote a dissertation on "The Dialectic of Truth and Freedom in Karl Jaspers" under the direction of Prof. James Collins. After teaching for two years in the Center for Thomistic Studies at the University of St. Thomas in Houston, he entered the Society of Jesus and was ordained in 1992. Since that time he has been teaching in the department of philosophy at Fordham University, where he is now an Associate Professor and regularly teaches courses in Natural Law Ethics. At Fordham he is also the Editor-in-Chief of *International Philosophical Quarterly*, directs the MA Program in Philosophical Resources, and serves as Chaplain and Tutor at Queen's Court Residential College for Freshmen.

Fr. Koterski will direct a session on natural law at the upcoming annual American Catholic Philosophical Association meeting, which begins on Friday November 3rd in Dallas, TX. Anyone interested in the Society and upcoming events should contact Joseph Koterski, Department of Philosophy, Collins Hall, Fordham University, Bronx, NY

NATURAL LAW SOCIETY

Est quidem vera lex recta ratio naturae congruens, diffusa in omnes, constans, sempiterna —Cicero

The Natural Law Society was founded in Basel, Switzerland, August 1979. Its purpose is to subject to critical examination the question of the existence of natural law and natural right, and their content and purpose. The Society is dedicated to strengthening the development of natural law/right philosophy and to understanding the relations between morals and the positive laws of nations and peoples. *Vera Lex*, the Society's review, was established to communicate and dialogue on the subject of natural law and natural right and to spread the education of natural law philosophy into the mainstream of contemporary thought; clarify and bring up to date its supporting ideas and to meet opposing argument with consistency and scholarly integrity; strengthen the current revived interest in the discussion of morals and law and advance its historical research.

CALL FOR PAPERS

"Liberalism & Natural Law"

It is almost a truism that "liberalism" (Kantian, Rawlsian *et al.*) based as it is on the supremacy and priority of the right over the good and holding as it does quotidian visions of social justice and the preferred life is incompatible with traditional natural law perspectives of self and community membership. Whereas 'individualistic' liberalism emphasizes an unencumbered self freed from constitutive ends, natural law requires a self situated within a common telos.

Having said this, are there fruitful points of contact, similarities between (neo) liberal and natural law approaches to social arrangements? Do individual and social agreements (*pactum societatis*) nullify natural rights? Can liberalism be communitarianized through natural law? Is there a common good in liberalism—such as neutrality and basic liberty—that holds a correspondingly central position in natural law? Can natural law theories be a catalyst for a renewed liberalism? These are just a few of the subjects you might want to consider for paper topics.

Deadline for submission is June 30th, 2001. Please address all manuscripts to Editor, *VERA LEX*, Pace University, Department of Philosophy and Religious Studies, 41 Park Row, New York, NY 10038.

AUTHORS WANTED FOR BOOKS ON NATURAL LAW

Editors of a Special Series of Books sponsored by Value Inquiry Books Series (VIBS), with the cooperation of the Natural Law Society and its publication VERA LEX, are pleased to invite prospective authors to submit original monographs and books on the subject of NATURAL LAW.

Publisher is Editions Rodopi
(Atlanta and Amsterdam)

For "Information for Prospective Authors" write to:

Vincent Luizzi
Chair and Professor
Department of Philosophy
601 University Drive
San Marcos, Texas 78666-4616
Off: 512-245-2285 Fax: 512-245-8335
VLUIZZI@swt.edu

www.ingramcontent.com/pod-product-compliance
Lightning Source LLC
LaVergne TN
LVHW090408210926
848480LV00002B/495
9780944473535